Libraries and the Handicapped Child

BOOKS BY THE SAME AUTHOR

Each According to his Ability:
a list of books and other visual
material for use by and with
mentally handicapped children (compiler)

Libraries and Literature for Teenagers

Seeing Clear:
books for the partially sighted child (compiler)

Libraries and the Handicapped Child

Margaret R. Marshall

MA, FLA

General Editor: Grafton Series

WESTVIEW PRESS
BOULDER, COLORADO

26.75 net

Published in 1981 in the United States of America by
Westview Press
5500 Central Avenue
Boulder, Colorado 80301

Frederick A. Praeger, Publisher

ISBN 0 86531 056 4

Library of Congress Catalog Card Number 80 51349

First published 1981 by
André Deutsch Limited
105 Great Russell Street London WC1

Published and distributed in India by
Clarion Books (Indian Book Company)
GT Road, Shadara, Delhi–110032

Printed in Great Britain by
Ebenezer Baylis & Son Limited
The Trinity Press, Worcester, and London

To my husband
Ronald McCondach McDonald
whose presence in my life is happiness

Contents

Preface

For some years now I have spent some of my leisure time with handicapped children and devoted some of my professional teaching and research to their reading needs. I have told stories and talked to and played with the children, conferred with their parents and teachers and tested both the content and the physical strength of books of all kinds.

I have visited special schools and organizations concerned with the care of handicapped children in several countries; drawn liberally on the small amount of printed information on libraries and the handicapped reader; read widely in the profuse literature on handicap, and now offer my thanks to all who have contributed to my knowledge and understanding of the theme of this book.

I acknowledge particularly the services of the libraries of the following: the School of Librarianship, Leeds Polytechnic; the Library Association, London; the Institutes of Education at the University of Leeds and the University of London; the Post-graduate Medical School, Pinderfields Hospital, Wakefield; and the International Youth Library, Munich; the staff of the special schools, Two Dales at Guiseley, Leeds and Woodside, Leeds; John Wheeler of the Hamilton Lodge School for the Deaf, Brighton; Henshaw School for the Visually Handicapped, Harrogate; Wrentham State School, Boston, USA; Vangede Children's Hospital School, Copenhagen and the Perkins School for the Blind in Harvard, USA. I also acknowledge the work of the many librarians who have produced lists of books for and about the handicapped child, and particular thanks go to Arleen M. Hynes, Chairperson of the Bibliotherapy Committee of the American Library Association, for the information and material she supplied.

It is hoped that the book will be of interest to librarians and teachers and that it will provide a source of reference and information for them in their work with handicapped children. Those who work in libraries in a particular field of handicap tend to acquire the necessary specialized knowledge over a period of time, by reading, conversation and experience. It may be that this book will impart some of that special knowledge, though provision of detailed information on every aspect of handicap is not the intention here.

Those who work in ordinary libraries to which handicapped children come, whether public or school libraries, may find this overview of the extraordinary needs of the special child useful as an introduction to some of the problems, which, hopefully, also provides some of the answers. Although the book is intended primarily for those with a basic knowledge of librarianship, it is hoped that parents of handicapped children will also find it of help in their attempts to satisfy their children's reading needs.

In most countries, each school, institution and library is different from the next, so that no blueprint is possible, or perhaps desirable, for library provision for handicapped children. What *is* possible, is an attempt to find common ground for libraries serving the distinctive needs of many handicapped children, while at the same time stressing the children's common normality. I hope I have succeeded, to the benefit of the children.

Margaret R. Marshall
December 1979

Chapter One

The size and nature of the problem

TWO CHILDREN out of every hundred are born with a severe defect requiring special education and treatment and a further 8 per cent have some degree of handicap. Such children have a greater degree of need when other stimuli and normal activity are denied.

How much effort should librarians give to that 10 per cent? The United Nations Statement on Rights says that the right to education and the right to read apply to all, whatever the condition of body or mind, whether at home, school or in an institution. The public library, one of the few open facilities for the population, has a vital part to play in filling the special needs of the handicapped child, and school libraries may be the first or only source of library aid for such children. The 1970 Chronically Sick and Disabled Persons Act, Section 2 (1b) states that there must be provided to the handicapped services which are equal to those the ambulant person could obtain.

Such official requirements are of little use unless librarians understand the needs of the handicapped and the nature of handicap.

The National Children's Bureau, in its publication *Living with Handicap*, has defined handicap as 'a disability which permanently, or for a substantial period, retards, distorts or adversely affects normal development or adjustment.'[1] Such a definition covers a wide variety of handicap including that of social deprivation and even giftedness. The various forms of handicap include:

1 Visual handicap, which includes the totally blind, those with residual vision and the partially sighted.
2 Hearing impairment, which includes the profoundly deaf, severely deaf and the partially hearing.
3 Physical handicap, which includes conditions such as spina bifida, cerebral palsy, chest and kidney conditions, congenital defects such as heart abnormalities, skin and muscular conditions, hydrocephalus and birth injuries, bone conditions, blood abnormalities, and injuries from road and other accidents.
4 Speech and language disorders not resulting from deafness, perhaps caused by organic defects of the nervous system or forms of aphasia, or defects such as cleft palates.
5 Epilepsy.
6 Intellectual and emotional handicap, which includes mental subnormality, educational subnormality, maladjustment, autism, personality and school phobia.
7 Multiple handicaps, which include the presence of more than one severe handicap. In addition to accompanying disorders, many handicapped children also suffer from intellectual and emotional problems as a direct result of their handicap.

Research on emotional disturbance in handicapped children reached the conclusion that:

> The evidence is striking that skilled psychological help and counselling should be available in all special schools. Families need help to deal with attitudes and feelings. The children, especially in adolescence, need opportunities to talk over, or for the less articulate, act out the difficulties of adjustment to adult life with a handicap. Finally the staff need easily available expert help in understanding the problems of the children in their care and in discovering the best ways of helping them.[2]

The number of children with a single handicap is decreasing as research experiments find new ways of preventing or curing certain handicaps, but many countries note that more children are being born with multiple handicaps. Some visually handicapped children have a degree of spasticity and some are also deaf; many deaf children have speech defects occasioned by their hearing handicap and many mentally handicapped children have physical disabilities. Many brain damaged children have severe physical dysfunctions, brain damage can include cerebral palsy, spasticity and epilepsy. There are around 12,000 such children in Britain of whom about 2,500 are severely mentally handicapped, the rest are of normal intelligence and mostly attend schools for the physically handicapped. One child in every 100 has some form of epilepsy and one child in every 300 has cerebral palsy to some degree. New disabilities are arising from the medical use of drugs, as in the case of thalidomide and vaccine damaged children.

However, the handicaps discussed in this book are those of usually physical or congenital origin, visual, hearing, speech, mental or physical handicaps, or, more commonly, a combination of these. The omissions include short-term hospitalized children, dyslexics, the emotionally disturbed, the gifted, and children with learning difficulties other than those caused by the handicaps specified. Social or environmental handicap is excluded from the study as being a large area requiring a book to itself, though it is a contributory factor to some handicaps and affects the quality of life and often the degree of aid available to the handicapped child and his family.

In Britain, the Department of Education and Science's *Education Statistics*[3] indicate that there are 1,870 special schools, 87 children's hospitals and 164 hospital schools, with 9,874 pupils and 1,138 full-time teachers in those hospital schools. The total number of handicapped children in education is broken down into the following categories:

Full-time pupils	
Blind and partially sighted	3,819
Deaf and partially hearing	7,015
Delicate and physically handicapped	18,442
Maladjusted	14,011
ESN(M) and ESN(S)*	84,044
Epileptic	2,252
Speech defects	6,908
Autism	542

* Educationally subnormal (mild) and educationally subnormal (severe).

In most countries where educationalists have concerned themselves with the needs of handicapped children there are national statements, some incorporated in legislation, some in reports, and there are local policies, and there is often a discrepancy between the two. There are also tremendous variations between the local administrative areas in matters of provision or policy. Such variations cause parents of handicapped children to feel victimized, or at least themselves handicapped, by the accident of geographical location. There are cases in a number of countries of parents moving house to an administrative area where there is better provision. While these variations are true for ordinary education, the child needing special education is doubly deprived if living in an educationally poor area.

This applies also to library authorities. The accident of birth in a particularly retarded or poor public library area further handicaps those who might have attempted to compensate for poor educational facilities by using the public library for self-education.

Although legislation in the library-conscious countries, such as the United Kingdom, the USA, the Scandinavian countries and Australia, specifies library service to all, as a continuing commitment, the degree of service to handicapped people tends to be a lesser priority for most state and local authorities and in some cases is non-existent in terms of policy or practice. Occasionally an individual librarian works wonders on a personal basis in her particular service area, despite the lack of policy, aid or encouragement from the library service hierarchy.

The handicapped child in school is discussed in the next chapter, but the tremendous variations between local administrative areas in matters of policy or provision, in every country, make it difficult to see an overall common pattern. However, in general, special schools have smaller school populations than most ordinary schools and a better staff/student ratio. In countries where there is a local centralized schools library service, facilities and materials are often available for 'special' needs but are not always exploited by either the service or the special schools. Most special schools have a large number of specialist non-teaching staff who attend to the special needs of the children. It has been estimated that about fifty people have some active responsibility for the welfare of one handicapped child, for instance, parents, teachers, education officers, physiotherapists, speech therapists, nursing sisters, psychiatrists, psychologists, training and employment officials, welfare and social workers, hospital/clinic staff, voluntary organizations staff, child care staff, the child's own doctor, and the librarian.

But what happens when the handicapped child becomes a teenager and must make plans for leaving school and for life as an adult? The mentally handicapped young person who is theoretically ineducable, may become educable with attention during childhood, but after leaving school he may regress to his pre-school state, and, through frustration, turn to aggression and self mutilation. Elizabeth Marais, in an article entitled 'Opening doors only to close them?',[4] argues the case for further education in colleges and centres. One such course is offered at Park Lane College of Further Education in Leeds, where the more able mentally handicapped people of sixteen to twenty can attend a variety of classes and also enjoy the library and storytelling.

The severely physically handicapped school leaver has few choices. If he is able to pursue academic higher education there are a few colleges specially for the physically handicapped, but many young people are not able to cope academically or physically with extended education courses in ordinary colleges. One college in Britain run by the Spastics Society, mainly for young people suffering from cerebral palsy, finds that about 25 per cent of its sixteen-year-old students have a reading age of twelve compared with 75 per cent of that age group in the wider community. As a result of using technical aids like talking books, reading machines and typewriters, language development and numeracy improve. Social and vocational skills are also developed to try to prepare the student for as independent a life as possible.

The academically-able, visually or hearing impaired school leaver also has a limited choice of academic or vocational further education, though many are trained as piano tuners, computer operators or telephonists, and many are able, with help, to pursue further education in ordinary colleges and universities. But for all handicaps, provision is very patchy in both Britain and America for the young person who is too old for school, but too *educationally* retarded for ordinary college.

Many public libraries offer help to people attending day care centres. One example is that of the Lambeth Special Care Unit in London, to which librarians go to read and tell stories and to generally liaise, with books as the shared factor. Those who are fortunate enough to have such a day centre available are often better served in this respect than those in residential centres.

Liaison is patchy between the various bodies concerned with the handicapped child. There are many research organizations specifically for a particular handicap and many general research departments in universities; voluntary organizations; funded societies; special teaching associations; medical associations concerned with handicap; commercial companies; the families of the children and the children themselves; all of whom want and need to know more about each other.

For all are pursuing the same objective – the right of the handicapped child to be accepted as a human being and to be given the same opportunities as the 'ordinary' child, and that includes the opportunity to benefit from books and a library service. The terms 'ordinary' and 'special' are used throughout this book to distinguish between those children who are not handicapped, and are therefore able to benefit from normal library and education services, and those children who are handicapped and therefore need special provision in both these areas.

Chapter Two

The handicapped child in school

SCHOOLING for the handicapped child has undergone many organizational changes in the last ten years and is still in the melting pot in several countries on the question of integration, or mainstreaming, of the 'special' child with the 'ordinary' child.

The England and Wales Education Act of 1976, Section 10, required local education authorities to arrange for the special education of all handicapped children to be given in county or voluntary schools, except where this was impracticable, incompatible with efficient instruction in schools or involved unreasonable public expenditure, in which case it could be given in special schools or, with the Secretary of State's approval, in independent schools.

The enforcement of this requirement was deferred to await the findings of the Warnock Report,[1] which, though it indicated that integration and improved provision in ordinary schools was a good thing, nevertheless considered that 'both day and boarding special schools will continue to be needed for children with moderate learning difficulties.'[2] The Act's requirements echoed the American legislation of 1975, the Education of All Handicapped Children Act, which recommended that handicapped children with exceptional needs should be educated in the least restrictive environment and that all others should be mainstreamed.

While the Warnock Report supported the concept of mainstreaming, it saw dangers in implementing this until staff, resources, understanding and curricula are available in ordinary schools. My own investigations on the eastern seaboard of the USA in 1979, revealed a widespread concern on the part of teachers and other educationalists, that though mainstreaming was good in theory, the special child was being failed by the system in many places for lack of adequately trained teachers knowledgeable about the special teaching and the special need, and lack of materials and equipment. For example, the mainstreaming of visually handicapped children in schools without a teacher able in braille, was resulting in children being denied the skill in braille reading and consequently becoming further disabled and retarded. Additional members of staff for the small group or one-to-one teaching required for educationally retarded children were not available either, so that disquiet was expressed about the implementation of mainstreaming without the necessary resources of staff and materials. An American teacher at an American airforce base in England also indicated that the presence of just one child with Down's Syndrome in his class caused him to spend a much greater proportion of his time on that one child than he could spare without neglecting the other children in the class.

How well the special child functions in integrated or mainstreamed schools is still open to conjecture and research, but the overall difficulty lies with the organizational methods and with the staff, rather than with the child. Such organization is open to a variety of practice.

The Warnock Report indicates the range of school provision as follows:

1 Full-time education in an ordinary class with any necessary help and support.
2 Education in an ordinary class with periods of withdrawal to a special class or unit or other supporting base.
3 Education in a special class or unit with periods of attendance at an ordinary class and full involvement in the general community life and extra-curricular activities of the ordinary school.
4 Full-time education in a special class or unit with social contact with the main school.
5 Education in a special class or unit, day or residential, with some shared lessons with a neighbouring day school.
6 Full-time education in a day special school with social contact with an ordinary school.
7 Full-time education in a residential special school with social contact with an ordinary school.
8 Short-term education in hospitals or other establishments.

9 Long-term education in hospitals or other establishments.
10 Home tuition.[3]

There are some children who are not able to attend either an ordinary or a special school, usually temporarily, sometimes permanently. Assessment is made by the school medical service and the head teachers of the relevant schools, in liaison with psychologists and welfare officers. The children are offered tuition by a teacher, or teachers, for a number of hours each week in their own homes, the amount depending upon the child's capacity, mental, physical and medical.

The children who need this kind of tuition may be those who have had a stay in hospital and now require a lengthy stay at home to convalesce; children who would normally be at school but are temporarily at home because they have behaviour problems, or are pregnant or have some form of temporary maladjustment; children who are severely physically handicapped and children who are severely mentally handicapped, with a physical disability also.

Many teachers suggest that the most profitable method of integration for the child who can be integrated, is that of placing him in the ordinary classroom with either extra resources being brought there or the child being taken to extra resources in the school. For most it is thought that education in a special unit on the main ordinary school campus is a helpful method, where the child is independently taught but shares most of the life and facilities of the campus.

Peripatetic or itinerant teachers are increasingly employed in several countries, including Britain and the USA. They are based at one school or unit but travel to other schools, units or home-taught children on a shared-time basis. This enables the handicapped child in an ordinary school to receive the specialist help he needs on a regular basis each week.

Whether education for handicapped children is mainstreamed or separated, a centralized advisory and service organization is necessary and helpful. In America, State Education Departments have a division concerned with special education and most have a Special Education Instructional Materials Center. In Britain, the local education authorities have a special education advisory team and though few have a special education materials centre, such material is often found in the local teachers centres and in the centralized schools library service in each authority. Similarly, in Australia the local education services Reading Centres contain remedial and special material.

The whole question of special versus integrated education has caused much controversy. A research project involving the USA, Denmark, Sweden and Britain,[4] noted that the polarization of thought, integration *versus* special schooling, was unnecessary, the two being complementary. It found nothing to strongly indicate the benefits of one or the other, and it seems that the pupils who were thought to be most successfully integrated had parents who were supportive in terms of encouraging a wide, active and independent life.

One of the conclusions of the research report was that many teachers in ordinary schools are ignorant of the disabilities and needs of the partially sighted child in their classes, and this lack of knowledge applies to all handicaps and most non-special education teachers, and results in apprehension, negative treatment or indifference. The same could be said of school librarians, hitherto not required to serve the needs of the special child.

Thus the special child in an ordinary school is possibly at risk if knowledgeable staff and appropriate resources are not available. The problem of possible fall-off in specialist care can also be seen in the findings of an experimental project initiated for the Institute for Research into Mental and Multiple Handicap in 1975.[5]

A resource centre on handicaps in children was established and offered to four London boroughs where educational integration was positive in both policy and practice. The service was aimed at health visitors, doctors, social workers, teachers, nursery nurses, welfare assistants and instructors, voluntary workers, speech therapists, occupational therapists and physiotherapists and hospital staff. Use was disappointingly low.

It was discovered that communication in many departments and organizations was poor, horizontally and vertically; that formal training on handicapping conditions for those caring for such people was most inadequate, and that few kept up to date with new developments, even in the specialized establishments and care professions.

> We were also astonished how few day-nursery staff had heard of the Toy Libraries Association or seen any simple stimulation toys which could be easily copied and developed with almost no cost. We were again repeatedly made aware of ignorance on the part of those working with handicapped children about the existence, let alone the work, of the many voluntary societies. Those in contact with the parents of handicapped children did not seem to read *Parents Voice* and so find out what parents think about their own problems. Those working in the special schools, even the teachers themselves, rarely seemed to read *Special Education*. Doctors read only medical journals, health visitors usually only nursing journals. This tends to perpetuate professional barriers and increases failure in inter-professional understanding and communication.[6]

It seems that librarians working in special education may be much better informed in that they tend to scan a variety of journals and documents concerning the speciality in the course of their work and it is part of their function to provide information or directions to information sources in the special field.

The research report recommended, amongst other things, multi-professional teams, better initial college education and subsequent in-service training, and the setting up of local resource centres on handicap, possibly on the integrated campus. Lack of information during initial training of teachers is apparent in most countries, except where the student teacher has made a specific choice to study for a specialist teacher's qualification.

I gave a guest lecture on books and the mentally handicapped child to a group of students studying education at a large university in Maryland and, though many of the students were deeply interested, many others said they would not be involved with mentally handicapped children in their future teaching career, this despite the fact that America has legislated for mainstreaming of handicapped children.

If integration or mainstreaming is to have any hope of being effective for the handicapped child, *all* student teachers and librarians must receive some guidance on the special needs of the handicapped, and in-service training must be given to staff who find themselves in integrated schools. If those concerned with the special care of handicapped children are not knowledgeable, the special child going into a non-special school will be in a very vulnerable position and will suffer if his particular, individual needs are not recognized and provided for.

To these comments could be added a further recommendation that librarians providing a service to children should also make it their business to attend courses and meetings on the special theme, both within their own profession and those concerned with handicaps, in order to be informed and updated.

Some years ago I organized a four-day residential course for children's and school librarians, which was oversubscribed. Attended by librarians from many parts of Britain, it provided information, involved group work, visited schools for the handicapped and enabled individual experiences to be shared. Similarly, in recent times the Library Association has organized short courses and one-day schools on various aspects of handicap and disadvantage. Some branches of organizations to which children's and school librarians belong, also pay attention to the theme. Most local education authorities have in-service courses and meetings for their special education teachers, which would also be of help to the librarians working with children in that district. I have twice addressed Regional Health Board in-service training courses for medical and para-medical staff, on the subject of books for handicapped children, and was pleased by the great interest shown in what was an almost unknown field to the one hundred doctors, nurses, therapists, health visitors and special education teachers present on each occasion.

The theme of the 1979 Youth Libraries Group of the Library Association's Weekend School, was 'The Other Child' and about two hundred librarians, publishers and writers attended the sessions, which covered the mentally handicapped, hearing impaired, gifted and rural child, books for all children via television, and the 'other' child in literature. Delegates were provided with much useful information to develop both attitudes and practices in the field of library service to handicapped children.

However, those who are interested enough to spend their own time (and usually their own money) attending such courses, are in the minority, a valuable minority, and systematic in-service training by employing authorities can be of value to all library staff who are likely to come into contact with the special child, his parents and those who work with the child.

Unfortunately, national legislation or local policy cannot always guarantee the provision of knowledgeable teachers and librarians, or the presence of a helpful attitude on the part of able children towards the inclusion of handicapped children in the ordinary school. In many countries the handicapped child is often the subject of hostility, resentment and ridicule, largely a result of the able child's lack of knowledge and awareness. There are, however, instances where integration has been successful, one of which is the Bicester School Progress Unit for ESN pupils aged eleven to sixteen.[7] This opened with fifteen children aged eleven to twelve and one teacher, in a building in the grounds of a big comprehensive school, the children being taught separately. But it was clear that playtime bullying occurred and the staff felt isolated. Over a period of six years a gradual integration took place, aided by a change in the main school teachers' attitudes. This in turn led to a change in the ordinary children's attitudes. Suitable materials for use in mainstream classes were provided, the children with intolerable behaviour or severe learning problems were given individual aid in the special unit, and twelve parents who had volunteered to help first-year children with their reading practice were encouraged and good relations were built up with them.

One of the problems facing teachers and librarians when providing materials, is that many handicapped children are *educationally* subnormal, below the normal level of knowledge and reading development for the chronological age range. In addition to educationally retarded children, there are, of course, those children with a mental retardation, but the label or description of 'slow learner' or 'child with learning difficulties' covers a wide range of disability. The following definitions and descriptions show the development of thinking on the subject:

> The educationally subnormal are children of limited ability and children retarded by 'other conditions' such as irregular attendance, ill health, lack of continuity in their education or unsatisfactory school conditions and who are retarded by more than 20 per cent for their age. They form 10 per cent of the school

population. Ministry of Education, pamphlet no. 5. *Special Educational Treatment*. London: HMSO, 1946.

The ESN are pupils who by reason of limited ability or other conditions resulting in educational retardation, require some specialized form of education wholly or partly in substitution for the education normally given in ordinary schools. Ministry of Education. *Handicapped Pupils in Special Schools*. Regulations 1959 as amended by Statutory Instrument 1973, no. 2021, Schools (Qualified Teachers) Regulations. London: HMSO, 1973.

This term is generally applied to children functioning educationally and cognitively below their chronological age. They frequently show problems on social performance as well. In England and Wales such children attend special classes in normal schools or ESN schools for either the mildly mentally handicapped (M) or the severely mentally handicapped (S). In North America these two groups closely correspond to the level of Educable and Trainable Mentally Handicapped respectively. Roy Brown. *Psychology and Education of Slow Learners*. London: Routledge & Kegan Paul, 1976.

. . . ESN children are usually identified by reference to educational criteria rather than medical or strictly intellectual criteria such as IQ levels. These educational criteria refer to standards of educational attainment (e.g. in reading and number) which correspond to those of children 20 per cent younger. Open University. *The Handicapped Person in the Community: providing supportive services*. Milton Keynes: Unit 11, Open University, 1975.

The educationally subnormal are children who have been ascertained as needing specialized education away from other children, in special schools and classes. They are assessed partly on IQ within the range 50–75. They are not to be confused with other children classified educationally subnormal severe with IQs generally speaking below 50. . . . the individuals within the group have different emotional and social needs. Boundaries are blurred . . . The one common element they have is that they have a limited response to normal education. The Elfrida Rathbone Society uses the term to describe . . . the young person who attends an ordinary school, who is in the lowest sections of the lowest streams and who has similar problems and needs to the educationally subnormal. The assumption that NERS makes is that the population of people who are educationally handicapped is larger

> than the number of children attending special schools. G. J. Johnson. *Information Sheet.* London: National Elfrida Rathbone Society, 1972.

> We suggest that, generally speaking, the characteristic of an educationally handicapped child is the ability to operate from Piaget's pre-operational or concrete operational stages, whereas the teacher of the Extra Educationally Handicapped (ESN.S) has to be prepared to begin at the sensory-motor stage of development. National Union of Teachers. Committee for Special Education. *The NUT View on the Education of Severely Subnormal Children.* London: NUT, 1972.

These variations in definition are minor compared with the major shift in emphasis over how to educate those so categorized, and the deliberations of the Warnock Committee were extensive on this point, beginning with the following statement:

> The term educationally subnormal is open to criticism on the grounds that it is imprecise and assumes agreement on what is educationally normal with regard to ability and attainment. It also suggests that a child so described suffers from an intrinsic deficiency whereas the deficiency has been in his social and cultural environment. We recommend that the term 'children with learning difficulties' should be used to describe both those children who are currently categorized as ESN and those with educational difficulties who are often at present the concern of remedial services. Mary Warnock. *Special Educational Needs: report of the Committee of Enquiry into the education of handicapped children and young people.* London: HMSO, 1978.

The Report goes on to suggest that children with sensory or physical disabilities, whether temporary or permanent, may well require not remedial help in the usual sense employed in British education, but possibly special help and support throughout their school lives.

Such special support involves an awareness of the fact that many handicapped children are educationally retarded because of a late start caused by hearing or visual impairment, or by low mental capacity, or because of hospitalization or treatment which interrupts schooling. It also involves an awareness of the style of teaching and librarianship required for most handicapped children, regardless of the kind of educational establishment. The search for appropriate methods has been considered by a number of educational philosophers, researchers and practitioners.

B. S. Bloom, in his 'Mastery of learning and its implication for curriculum development', says that:

> The normal curve in grading pupils expects about 10 per cent at each extreme and the curriculum both actual and hidden, the teaching methods, and the teacher and pupil expectations are all conditioned rather than designed to perpetuate this . . . Aptitude is the amount of time required by the learner to attain mastery of a learning task. Thus aptitudes are predictive of the rate rather than level (or complexity) of learning that is possible . . . The problem is to find ways of reducing the amount of time required by the slower students to a point where it is no longer a prohibitively long and difficult task for those less able students.[8]

Subnormality or delayed normality is seen by Haskell, Barrett and Taylor as affecting slow children's intellectual and reading development 'because they do not employ an appropriate strategy when obliged to extract meaning from the ceaseless input of information from the environment. They are slow learners because they have not learnt to focus attention on the relevant aspects of the stimuli, or to withdraw attention from excessive information.'[9]

What then is recommended for those teachers and librarians who must organize teaching and learning in order to mitigate, overcome or use the causes of reading retardation? What strategies are suggested by educationalists for enabling the special child to learn more successfully? Teachers should:

> . . . guard against overloading the information . . . children perform best when information is presented, controlled and issued in manageable units . . . repetition and practice to consolidate previously learned materials is strongly indicated and the risk of random learning minimized by avoiding unnecessary alternative choices in learning tasks.[10]

Many handicapped children cannot know what is relevant or irrelevant in information, in tasks set or in the stimuli around them, and need to have the relevant presented to them in a structured way, proceeding from the known to the known, and then from the known to the unknown, by means of vocabulary, concepts and materials which are significant, with activities being organized and directed into specific channels.

The inclusion of a reward in the teaching programme has been seen to achieve both pupil satisfaction and subsequent motivation with the ordinary child. Boocock, in his *Introduction to the Sociology of Learning*,[11] noted that praise like 'good' and 'fine', produced the greatest improvements in performance among lower socio-economic status children, while middle-class children were more susceptible to reinforcers connoting correctness, e.g. 'right'. Much work is done with brain damaged and mentally handicapped children by means of offering tangible rewards and in all cases this is accompanied by verbal praise and approval of success. In most cases a reward system can achieve behaviour modification *and* development of knowledge or skills.

My own experience of book sessions with emotionally disturbed children in care, proved that the promise of, for example, a piece of chocolate, enabled hyperactive and disruptive children to remain still and attentive long enough to listen and learn enough to justify the system, and lavish praise was given for any evidence of co-operation and knowledge. This encouraged motivation to behave, and therefore learn, on the next occasion.

Samuel A. Kirk and G. Orville Johnson, writing as long ago as 1911,[12] included the following in their recommendations for stimulating motivation, and these are just as valid today:

1 Provide understandable materials.
2 Make the child aware of success.
3 Encourage the child to compete with himself against previous achievement.
4 Provide easy/interesting reading materials.
5 Provide a large variety of books.
6 Encourage wide reading for information.
7 Allow children to select.
8 Vitalize through visual aids.
9 Encourage the reading of newspapers.

10 Provide opportunities for sharing items/news/stories etc.
11 Have a bulletin board or magazine.

Though originally advocated as a reading programme for the mentally handicapped child, the basic features of Kirk and Johnson's programme are applicable to all children retarded in their reading. Four areas are suggested: a reading readiness programme, a prolonged beginning reading period, a programme which develops methods of word recognition and efficiency in independent reading, and definite guidance in the comprehension of more complex reading materials. The reading readiness programme is described as:

1 Excursions, etc.
2 Making and labelling collections.
3 Making equipment and collecting books.
4 Storytelling by librarian, teacher and other children.
5 Story reading.
6 Informal discussion.
7 Associating words with pictures.
8 Dramatization.
9 Booklets and scrapbooks.
10 Kinds of and care of books.
11 Playing games with numbers, language, colour, home, garden, jobs.
12 Information for bulletin board or magazine.
13 Telephone conversation.
14 Drawing pictures.[13]

While these are normal kindergarten and primary school methods, they have a special significance and emphasis in the teaching of the reading retarded child, whatever the cause of retardation, and whether in classroom or library, for the liaison between teacher and librarian, between classroom and library, is crucial.

Whether in a special school or mainstreamed school, the librarian must ensure that the information needed to provide an effective library service is obtained. He needs to know the level of reading ability, the reading interests, and the subject requirements of the special child; the areas of professional concern of the teaching staff, in order to supply them with special materials, both for teaching purposes and for updating their information concerning the handicap; and he also needs to take account of the possibilities of using non-print materials with some categories of handicap, and with all children who have difficulty with print. My own research into this has shown that it is possible to get across by audio-visual or non-print means, information otherwise denied the child who cannot read.

Conveying the printed word from the page and into the minds of children by means of storytelling or story reading, is an important feature of any library for children and young people, and is commonly employed in special schools but not so often in ordinary high schools, it being considered that the 'normal' child leaves behind such a 'childish' thing as storytime when he reaches the age of twelve or so. The chapter on storytelling looks at the emphases which facilitate understanding and enjoyment for the special child, but here it is necessary to look at storytelling and book sessions as part of the librarian's school/teaching function.

Most public librarians who go into secondary schools to talk about books, tell or read a suitable story or excerpt as part of their talk. Some teachers read aloud stories other than the novels being studied and some school librarians are able to do this also, but it becomes particularly important to the mainstreamed child, probably used to it and needing it in his previous special school, to continue to benefit from the reading aloud of books which it is likely he could not tackle on his own. He may not be able to go to public library story sessions and thus misses out on an opportunity to mix with other children.

Integration is aided by voluntary schemes such as that which I initiated with a group of handicapped children over a continuous period of six years. Contact with a local special school led me to offer to read and tell stories to the children on a weekly basis at the school. This developed into an arrangement whereby the children, aged twelve to thirteen, were brought by mini-bus to me at my college of librarianship, every Wednesday afternoon, to widen their experience.

Eventually a dozen or so were coming by public transport with a teacher, for the social experience, having a story from me as a group, and then pairing off with one of my students for half an hour of reading, conversation and building up a personal relationship, followed by a glass of orange and a biscuit. Interest was intense, behaviour problems rare and enjoyment of books visible. The few who had any reading ability were encouraged to practise it, all the books used were picture books, but there was no overt teaching, and no pressure put on any child to read. Most were enthralled by the opportunity to have the individual attention of the student and sole right to an enjoyable book during the reading of it, and each gloried in the right to choose the book from a selection and carry it to his helper student.

In this example the integration into 'normal' society was by mixing with people outside the school who were (a) older; the students were nineteen to twenty-one, (b) not teachers; I was not considered a teacher because I was not on the staff of their school, and (c) reached by going to them on a public bus, itself a difficult feat for these children, who at the age of twelve were not adept at handling money or knowing when to get off the bus, or even at sitting properly on bus seats. The use of volunteers in this way is largely unexplored by teachers or librarians and, though time consuming to organize, provides benefits which I amplify later in the chapter on storytelling.

For the librarian in an ordinary school there are difficulties in providing the same quantity and range of material in suitable content and format for the mainstreamed handicapped child as he would have expected and received in his special school. The cost of providing the appropriate material for the one or two or handful of special children, is out of all proportion from a budget viewpoint. Whereas in the special school the expenditure would be cost-effective in terms of numbers of users, in the mainstreamed school it would be difficult to give the handicapped child the same quantity and range to fit his needs and it would also require an expenditure of time. The extraction of appropriate materials from amongst the full range may require additional cataloguing, and possibly extra guiding, advice and liaison.

Such expenditure of time is a problem in the many schools where a teacher administers the library in addition to his teaching load. Even in a special school library such time would be difficult to find. The American *Standards for Library Services for the Blind and Visually Handicapped*[14] recommend the employment of a full-time qualified librarian for each hundred students after the first 100. While this is unlikely in all but the large special schools or mainstreamed schools with a special unit, it indicates the proportion of time that a librarian would need to allocate to provide a helpful service to handicapped children and their special staff in the ordinary school library.

The school librarian in an ordinary school needs to pay attention to matters which may not have concerned him when the school did not serve handicapped children. The question of physical access to, and mobility within, the library is detailed in the chapter on planning, but in general the ordinary school library should be inspected for hazards or inconveniences to the special child; access for wheelchairs, height of shelves and tables; physical availability of hardware and software for audio-visual materials and the space to use them; special lighting in particular areas; provision of large and clear print and colourful information via posters, charts and instruction sheets for those with a visual impairment, a requirement for appeal to an ordinary child also.

The chapter on selection gives examples of special materials, as do the sections concerned with specific handicaps, but the integration of the visually handicapped as shown in articles on the theme, requires stress to be laid on the involvement of the librarian, special teachers and other teaching staff in the selection of appropriate materials. In 'Blind children learn to relate',[15] liaison with the parents and the public library is stressed and the need for large print catalogue cards and braille is also mentioned.

Involving all the children in an integrated school with the problems and practices of the visually handicapped children is another aspect, and this is described in Ruth M. White's 'Light in a dark world'. Writing about her library service to visually handicapped children in her ordinary school, she suggests that the entire school population can be encouraged to produce projects, topics or term papers on the problems of the handicap, for example:

> With the junior and senior high school groups the librarian can suggest . . . the history of braille writing, the seeing eye dog program [guide dogs in Britain], the hygiene of the eyes, library services to the blind, talking books, new optical aids for the

> partially sighted and similar subjects covering many basic interests ... the school's library club members or members of other school service groups may vote to serve as volunteer readers for the school's visually handicapped children.[16]

The use of volunteer readers and mobility helpers presents no problems as many volunteer children show patience, interest and perseverance in this matter. The special child may have been used to this in his special school, where it is the custom for the more able to help the less able whatever the handicap. While special topics on handicaps are feasible, whether studied in social studies, health, English or library lessons, they nevertheless present the problem of locating the sources of such information, requiring the librarian to obtain the relevant materials to support the study of these themes. Bob Jerrolds suggests in an article on 'Preparing librarians to help the disabled reader', that the librarian asks the handicapped child reader to read a page aloud. 'If five words per page are missed it is probably too difficult. Librarians usually vastly overestimate the reading levels of the remedial student.'[17] While the provision of support materials for a study of handicapping features, and of material for both the handicapped and the ordinary student, requires a knowledge of reading abilities, such a course of action to determine ability should not be undertaken without looking carefully at the degree of privacy available for this 'test'; the nature of the handicap; the kind of book and the purpose for which it is required; and whether the ordinary child is also tested in this way. The article also contains the warning that the disabled reader may know how to use the card catalogue, but may not be able to read the cards, notices, directions, etc, and the recommendation that the librarian should encourage greater use of audio-visual materials with the disabled reader.

Two American school librarians advise on the teaching aspects necessary for librarians to be effective with the special child in their midst. One suggests getting each child interested by expelling fears about asking for help, by keeping everything simple in the beginning, increasing complexity as the children become more competent, by encouraging them to voluntarily try different facilities and by engaging the full co-operation of the staff with regard to library materials and use.[18]

In the second example, an ordinary elementary school has

about one hundred special pupils to whom the school's Instructional Materials Center librarian gives special attention, with instruction on the use of the catalogue, and on individual selection of print and audio-visual materials, using parental help and liaising with the teaching staff.

> All school media librarians recognize the necessity of co-ordinating activities and programs with what occurs in the classrooms. With children who have some sort of impaired learning ability this is crucial, for it is through repetition that they learn. A conceptual approach organizing units of study around a certain theme, reinforcing classroom activity with field trips is most successful . . . Because of their unique needs, some special children have almost totally individualized instruction . . . and must learn to listen attentively as members of a group. The Instructional Materials Center is a perfect place for reinforcing this skill. During group time the concept that books are a source of pleasure is also introduced.[19]

The librarian's assistance in ordinary and special school libraries may also take the form of helping the child to physically take the books from the shelf and put them through the charging system, perhaps carrying the books or placing them in bags, reading aloud the posters and notices and using the catalogue with the child if he has digital or reading difficulty, and perhaps making special arrangements for materials for home use.

The importance of liaising with teachers and parents for two-way information is stressed by all librarians working with special children, for, without careful co-ordination and attention to detail on the part of the many individuals and organizations concerned with his care, it is all too easy for the mainstreamed child to lose out.

Bringing the special child into the mainstream of education and society is the result of certain objectives (a) to minimize the 'otherness' feeling, (b) to normalize education and socialization, and (c) to develop the potential and to fit the child for an independent life in the adult world.

While these are valid objectives, they are not exclusive to mainstreaming as they pertain also to the special schools for those children with severe handicaps who need more special care than can be given in the ordinary school. The objectives are, of course, also valid for ordinary schools and the education of the ordinary child. That this is so, is an indication of the recognition of the overall normality of a handicapped child, the special aspects in teaching and library matters being a question of degree or emphasis rather than difference.

Some of the emphases are common to all handicaps, others are peculiar to an individual disability. For convenience, all are looked at in each of the sections devoted to an individual handicap and then later repeated where a common factor is evident. One factor stands out, that the librarian and the handicapped child in school need each other for the maximum effectiveness of the library in the education of the child.

Chapter Three

The mentally handicapped child and the library

THE TERM mentally handicapped covers children with varying kinds of disability, such as mongolism or Down's Syndrome, spastic conditions, brain damage, and hydrocephalus. The handicap range is wide, from slight to severe, and there are many grossly subnormal and multi-handicapped children.

Statistics show that one in every 100 children is born with a degree of mental handicap and recent trends have attempted to educate and train the children to a much higher level than was previously thought possible, though not without difficulty.

The 1959 British Mental Health Act defines mild handicap as a 'state of arrested or incomplete development of mind' and severe handicap as 'incapable of living an independent life or of guarding himself against serious exploitation.'[1]

The inclusion of autism in this section is done with the full knowledge that autistic children are not necessarily mentally handicapped in the sense of being mentally retarded, but are handicapped by a condition which causes them to be emotionally very young (apparent at the pre-school stage intellectually), physically lagging behind normal contemporaries and socially often inadequate.

Though healthy and often attractive in appearance, they have special difficulties, are often either withdrawn and apathetic or hyperactive, and appear disinterested in people and surroundings, but may exhibit unusual interest in inanimate objects.

In Britain there are about 6,000 such children, a little less than figures for blind children and about the same as those for deaf children. But only about 5 per cent get the very specialized education needed.

The National Society for Autistic Children in America states that surveys reveal a general incidence of about four in every 10,000 children, autism occurring more frequently in males. Its publicity material stresses that it is a mistake to think of the autistic child as deaf or mentally retarded, an understandable mistake given the behavioural characteristics of autism. Some autistic children do eventually learn socially acceptable behaviour and some do master reading, writing and arithmetic, though most can only be helped towards better communication, socialization and occupation. Though they may never be able to read a text for pleasure they can enjoy pictures, recognizing words, and using some information books.

Some diagnoses of mental handicap are based on IQ (Intelligence Quotient) tests and the following indicate the variations:

USA		*UK*		*World Health Organization*	
Mild	55–69	Mild	50–70	Mild	52–56
Moderate	40–54	Severe	below 50	Moderate	36–57
Severe	25–39			Severe	25–35
Profound	below 25			Profound	below 25

These need to be compared with average IQs which put various categories of employment into particular IQ brackets, for example, casual labouring 82, unskilled work 87, semi-skilled 98, skilled manual 109, higher manual/technical executives 117, lower professional technicians and executives 132, higher professionals and administrators 153, with the average able pupil at around 115 and the university graduate at about 125.

But the weaknesses inherent in using IQ are well known, being related to language, deprivation, social and intellectual factors. Some other tests are considered more accurate, for example, Weschler Intelligence Scale for Children (WISC), the Dutch Snijders-Ooman Test and the Cerebrezze Grouping.

The number of mentally handicapped people in the United Kingdom is about 200,000 with a further estimated 28,000 born each year.

The children's education and care is divided between hospital, where 7,000 live permanently, special schools, where approximately 20,000 are educated, and the child's own home, where about 6,000 are permanently based. These are all usually termed educationally subnormal severe (ESN. S). Add to these the approximately 85,000 mildly educationally subnormal (ESN. M) children and the scale of the handicap is evident.

It is important to distinguish between the mentally handicapped who will always be handicapped, and the mentally ill, who may be cured and are therefore likely to be temporarily handicapped. The fact that the two are often together in hospital is a matter of past history in the United Kingdom and present necessity, in the absence of suitable alternative accommodation and care.

Of the children in hospital, about one-third are severely mentally subnormal, one-sixth are educationally subnormal and the rest have psychopathic disorders. In a report on children in hospitals for the subnormal,[2] it was stated that 23 per cent had additional physical handicaps. It also noted a wide difference between hospital routine and boarding school or residential home routine, in the effect on language. This aspect was graphically described in an article called 'Unlocking the doors',[3] which forcefully put forward the case for hostels rather than hospitals for the mentally handicapped.

But what are the causes of mental handicap? The most common form of mental handicap is mongolism or Down's Syndrome, caused by an extra chromosome. Some retardation is caused by German measles during pregnancy, some by chemical disorders which produce abnormality before birth. Blood group incompatibilities may cause brain damage before birth and damage may occur during birth. Environmental and genetic factors are also causes.

The features of mental handicap include, at worst, hyperactivity, self-directed aggression, aggression against others, destructiveness, anxiety or depression, withdrawal, and psychotic fears or obsessions. On average mentally handicapped children are emotionally very young, with poor physical co-ordination and speech or communication difficulties. They are often socially and physically retarded, or physically disabled, with a poor concentration span, and, in the case of many children with Down's Syndrome, a very affectionate nature.

Severely retarded children suffering from cerebral palsy pose problems to those who try to assess their mental and intellectual level or the degree of their learning ability. The problems are those of establishing communication with a child with minimal speech, limited hand control and severely limited attention span, possibly with hearing difficulties, some vision defect and who may, understandably, be emotionally disturbed. Such severely handicapped children need long-term assessment and education and a rare example of such an assessment centre is that of Hawksworth Hall, near Guiseley in Yorkshire, England, which is operated by the Spastics Society for about thirty children aged five to twelve. The staff of forty-four includes teachers, physiotherapists, classroom assistants, speech therapists, house parents, domestic helps, handymen and clerical staff.

Not all cerebral palsied children have such severe disabilities nor are they all mentally handicapped, but most have a degree of retardation educationally.

The possible effect of mental handicap on reading and library use is being studied by a committee of the National Book and Library Centre (NBLC) in the Netherlands. Using the international classification of mentally handicapped people, the Celebrezze Grouping, according to the severity of the handicap, consideration is being given to the possibility of its application to book selection. The groupings are borderline retardation, mild mental retardation, moderate, severe, and profound mental retardation. The committee has tried to determine 'book behaviour' and reading and mental ages for each category. It may be that the demarcation lines are too soft and the variables too many and that librarians should be aware of the classifications, rather than apply them to book selection.

Certainly, practice varies considerably from country to country in the organization of education for the mentally handicapped child and in the style of education adopted for each category.

In the UK the severely subnormal child may attend a special school financed by the state, either as a day pupil or a boarder; he may be in a special unit, he may be in a hospital school as a day pupil or as a resident, he may be at a fee-paying special school as a day pupil or a resident, or he may be at home.

In just a few places it is possible for the mentally handicapped teenager who has reached the school leaving age, to continue his education at a college or a day centre. Those who are able to, can work in sheltered workshops, attend training centres or hold a job in the local community.

In most schools for the mentally handicapped, greater emphasis is placed on developmental and social skills than on academic skills. For instance, cultivating habits and skills to enable the child to be socially acceptable; teaching him how to live with others and be useful; developing use and understanding of language; encouraging pride in appearance; creating an atmosphere of affection and achievement; making him as able as possible to fit into 'normal' life; contributing towards self-help and independence if possible.

Some of the children resident in an institution are too severely handicapped for academic teaching. One writer suggests that the purposes of education for those children are:

1 To assist the inmate to lead an enjoyable life within the institution.
2 To help and direct the formation of good habits and positive attitudes.
3 To bring out individual aptitudes and abilities, to stimulate interests relevant to these attributes.
4 To develop potential working proficiency.
5 To encourage the inmates to think for themselves and become more independent.[4]

Some schools offer detailed instruction on social subjects like sex education. Here the school and/or public library may be called upon to provide books and other media to support the classroom teaching.

Lakeside School for the Mentally Handicapped, Welwyn Garden City, Hertfordshire, teaches sex education via children making plaster models; visits from mother and baby clubs; animals; counselling parents and teachers before the girls reach puberty; visual aids and Schools Broadcasting television programmes; and discussion with pupils arising from their remarks.[5]

Many behave like young teenagers and the school believes that this subject should be undertaken before moving on to adult training centres. Teachers and parents may seek advice in libraries about suitable books, and librarians need to be aware of sources of very simple textual and illustrative information. This is mentioned in the chapter on book selection.

The great majority of mentally handicapped children are not able to read for pleasure in the sense of imaginative cerebral enjoyment, nor can the majority expect to read fluently enough to cope with normal books, either children's or adults'. Some children, however, do develop an interest, enthusiasm and ability to read and profit from books, against great odds, which astounds and confounds the 'experts' and delights the parents, for such results, rare though they are, are usually produced by a caring individual or family.

The best known example of recent years is that of Cushla, a little girl in New Zealand whose parents and grandparents surrounded her with books and conversation and took her from a state of being a multi-handicapped baby to a happy young girl, able to communicate in particularly descriptive language, and to read with a deep love of books, though still handicapped in many ways. The extraordinary story is documented in Dorothy Butler's moving book, *Cushla and Her Books*,[6] which should be required reading for every parent, teacher and librarian concerned with a handicapped child, detailing as it does, not only the progress of the handicap, but the changing scores on numerous tests; the family life; the reading experience; the conversations, and, above all, the effects of a concentrated, intensive and genuine love and sharing of books with Cushla.

In an article in *Parents Voice*,[7] Margaret Polack describes similar perseverance, dedication and enthusiasm, in her efforts to give her mongol daughter Ruth the extra stimulation needed to enable her to live as normal a life as possible. So successful were the family's efforts with speech, vocabulary and reading, that Ruth's vocabulary increased rapidly until 'by six, she was speaking in proper sentences with conjunctions.' Her mother taught her to read at five, using the Teach Your Baby to Read scheme, then the Ladybird Key Readers, until, at nine years of age, 'she has a reading age of her chronological age.'

While such quantities of effort, teaching and books are not the norm in the home or school of the mentally handicapped child, most schools do provide a range of books in classrooms and/or libraries, and books do play a large part in school programmes.

At the newly built, attractively designed, Two Dales School

at Guiseley, Leeds, under the direction of the dynamic head teacher Gladys Vause, books are displayed, front facing where possible, in book racks, and are used by pupils and staff for class work, reward, leisure reading and storytime. Much of the stock consists of the simplest picture books and Roger Hargreaves' *Mr* books are immensely popular. Ladybird books, reading schemes and a selection of picture books provide a range of reading and viewing material complemented by storytime, finger play, music and singing. The children produce a school magazine with simple drawings and texts, mostly recording their daily activities. There is an air of purpose, cohesion and caring about the whole school and a close relationship between teachers and parents. Though the school is too small to support a librarian, each member of staff has an interest in the use of reading material.

Practice varies in different countries as to whether the degree of severity of mental handicap dictates whether a child should live at home and attend such a day school, or whether he should be resident in a school or hospital. In Denmark, the children's hospital for mentally handicapped children, in Copenhagen, caters for residential and day pupils and is fortunate in having a small library room and a qualified librarian who works twenty-two hours a week, during which time the library is open for use.

It is an attractive room, about fifteen feet by twenty-five feet, shelved on three sides to a height of six feet. The multi-coloured picture books are attractively displayed and the shelves have large markers to indicate the alphabetical location of the books. A collection of cassettes, slides, kits, charts, illustrations and laminated pictures complements the book stock and all are heavily used by teachers and children at the hospital. As the consultant and medical staff use an adjoining room for consultations with parents, the library is also useful for occupying the children during the discussions with visiting parents, and all can browse and borrow. The four hundred or so books are largely simple picture and information books, some of which are suitable for teenage interest and for school work. The visual material is used a great deal by teachers, both to impart information, and to promote communication with the children.

When I visited the library in 1979, the librarian, Susanne Holst, was enthusiastic about her work with the children and the staff, but recognized that more time and/or staff were needed to really develop the service to the full. She has written articles and reports in Danish, on the theme of books and libraries for the mentally handicapped child and the Danish Library Bureau has published her list of suitable picture books.

At the other extreme, I have visited mental institutions where there is no library for the children; where violent and disturbed children are locked away, sometimes in adult wards; where the special units for grossly handicapped children concentrate solely on the physical aspects of keeping the children clean, fed and comfortable and where the teachers in the hospital school each have their own locked cupboard with books they use with the children in their care. At one such hospital the reasons given for the absence of a library and the closely guarded staff-only books, were the likely damage to books if children had access to them and the lack of finance to buy anything but the basics. I commented on this to a head teacher of a special school where there were some children as badly affected as some at the hospital school, and she was certain that the whole question of damage (except in the case of children prone to extremely violent behaviour) was conditioned by the attitudes of the people concerned with the children. She believed that caring for things was something that could be taught, and in her school it was taught, even to the profoundly handicapped. It was part of the whole collective policy and attitude of the school and of the individual teachers.

As with physically handicapped children, inadvertent damage to books may occur, and there is a need to consider possible damage, particularly to those books which are on loan via the centralized schools library service. But the use of print and non-print materials by handicapped people is common at many places of library provision, for instance, at the Wrentham State School near Boston, Massachusetts, where there are 1,100 residents of whom 400 are non-ambulatory and 130 are children. Many of these use the large library which is open all day.

The full-time librarian, Trudy Innes, promotes the stock, which covers books of varying difficulty, including the Touch and Tell Books published by the American State Printing House. There are also 25 movie films, 200 filmstrips, 1,000 games, 2,000 cassettes and records and musical toys and puppets.

The librarian encourages the use of headsets and carrels to enable the library users to pursue their favourite pastime of listening to music. Teachers and therapists use the library both with and without the residents. When I visited the library in 1979, there were a number of different activities taking place – a man browsing through the books, a mongol girl reading a book with a teacher in one of the carrels, a brain damaged, physically disabled girl with headphones listening to a story, a mongol teenage boy happily listening to a record on headphones and humming along with the music, and the librarian busily preparing materials for addition to stock. With the help of two part-time assistants, the librarian offers a valuable and appreciated service in an attractively furnished and decorated library, for a community on a very large campus in an isolated district. However, the librarian is not isolated in the sense that liaison is maintained with the co-ordinating body, the Bureau of Library Extension in Boston.

Those who provide books for, and use books with, mentally handicapped children are confronted with the problem of selection which involves, as always, (a) knowing the needs of the children, (b) identifying the criteria that will satisfy them, (c) locating the books that will match the criteria, and (d) obtaining the books. I attempted this in my publication *Each According to his Ability: a list of books and other visual material for use by and with mentally handicapped children.*[8] In America there are many such lists, one example being the booklet produced by the Exceptional Children's Division of the Public Library of Cincinnati and Hamilton County, covering books for different age groups of the educable mentally retarded children and some for the trainable retarded. In the USA, educable means mild and borderline retardation, with an IQ between 55 and 80, whereas trainable mentally retarded means severe and moderate retardation, with an IQ between 25 and 54. In Britain the educational terms used for the equivalent division would be ESN(M) and ESN(S).

In Norway, Tordis Ørjasæter has written *Boka on Dag Tore*,[9] in Denmark Susanne Holst's list is published by the Danish Library Bureau, and she and I, and Sancia Simonis-Rupert of the Netherlands Book and Library Centre, at The Hague, are co-operating on a pamphlet for IFLA (International Federation of Library Associations), a joint effort of the Children's Libraries Section and the Hospital Libraries and Handicapped Readers Section of IFLA.

But one of the problems of selecting books for the mentally handicapped child lies in the need for familiarity, and recommended titles suitable for one country or even one part of a country are not likely to be suitable for another when, for instance, dress, architecture, customs, language and facial appearance are different. However, there are subject themes and physical design and layout requirements, which are common for all mentally handicapped children of whatever nationality, and these are indicated in the chapter on selection criteria rather than here, because they apply also to other types of handicap, particularly hearing impairment and children with learning difficulties. A few titles are mentioned there to exemplify points, but there is no attempt to provide lists, either selective or exhaustive, the former being available in many countries, the latter being impossible. The best practice is to apply the known criteria to selection amongst whatever source of books is available to the selector.

In addition to the normal commercially produced books, tactile, visual, scratch and sniff material, rag and cloth books, pictures, objects and audio-visual materials are desirable for children who have poor digital control, clumsy movements and possible eye defects, plus those with spastic conditions, all of whom may have difficulty in turning pages.

How do mentally handicapped children use books? From children known to me I recall Stephen, brain damaged and multi-handicapped. At the age of eight he is unable to walk and drags himself along the floor or is carried by his mother, a small slender woman who is little bigger than Stephen. His arms are deformed and partially paralysed but he 'helps' his parents to turn the pages of the books he loves to look at, particularly those to do with cars.

Jenny, a mongol girl now aged ten, is severely affected and has a hole in the heart. From babyhood she was introduced to books by her three sisters and her mother, and loves to lie on the floor looking at books, using her whole hand to rush at the pages, either to 'point' to something or to try to turn the page.

She is only interested in books that contain pictures of things that are familiar to her and 'reading' for her is the apparently enjoyable experience of recognizing these.

John is an eighteen-year-old mongol boy whose family have done everything possible to train him, integrate him, and prepare him for adult life. In school, I watched him while he read from a reading scheme book, of the level of reading age eight. He read hesitantly but accurately, and though he was able to answer some questions to verbally test his comprehension of the passage he had read, it was evident that he possessed to some degree that facility that all readers have, an ability to read aloud anything put in front of them, including scientific or language material, without the ability to understand what is read.

His own choice of books included the *Mr* books by Roger Hargreaves, and he was also interested in pictorial non-fiction, contributed to the school magazine and was considered to be capable of holding a very simple job in the community when he left school.

David, aged eleven, in a hospital school, brain damaged and with poor eyesight, was destructive towards books and people. Those escaping this treatment were his particular teacher and what David called 'the Monster books', which were the Dr Seuss books. He loved the rhythm of the text and the shapes and colours of the creatures.

And of course there is the rare case of Cushla, already mentioned, multiply handicapped, much of whose vocabulary was taken directly, unchanged, from the books her family read to her.

> Often a phrase or sentence 'takes over' when Cushla starts to talk e.g. 'there's a cat . . . to sit on the doorstep or purr by the fire' (from *The Little Wooden Farmer*) almost as if the words slip out unbidden. She gets in first while listening to *Make Way for Ducklings* by Robert McCloskey, with 'a great responsibility' and 'bursting with pride', phrases which are used to describe the duck parents' attitudes to the new ducklings. Cushla's expression, a model of expansive satisfaction, leaves no doubt that these phrases, unheard several weeks ago, have acquired meaning and will be available for use before long in other contexts.[10]

But books and reading for information purposes are only one

medium and games, toys, cassettes and film materials all contribute towards stimulating the mind and exercising the eyes and the hands of the handicapped child. Television plays a part too.

In Britain, the BBC programme *Let's Go*, a series of programmes for the mentally handicapped, is aimed at developing the independence of the individual and is screened twice a week, first as part of the Schools Broadcasting Service. The second showing gives viewers an opportunity to see the programme if they missed it the first time, and also helps to reinforce learning by repeating the viewing.

Let's Go Shopping, *Let's Go to the Post Office*, *Let's Telephone*, indicate the educational/socialization nature of the programmes. Handicapped people are shown carrying out the procedures to be learned and two presenters, male and female, reinforce the message by word and deed, co-ordinating sight and sound. A cartoon character is used also; thus the information is transmitted three or four times in different ways, by different people, using language both spoken and visual, sounds appropriate to the actions or equipment shown, and colour, movement and actions in visual form. All these conform to the recommended teaching skills mentioned in the previous chapter as being necessary for use with educationally retarded children. A package of print material using the words and phrases, and symbols and drawings from the television series, is available for use with the programme or independently.

The themes are those which are needed in books: colour, number, size, weight, time, speed, people, animals, houses, schools, hospitals, transport, and things that are relevant to the experience, such as environment, activities, fears, and emotions. They must also be relevant to the literal minds of the children who may grow into adulthood physically, but who retain the mind of a child.

Library service to such children, whether in school, hospital or public library, contributes towards raising the 'ceiling' of achievement, developing the potential that every child has, and providing enjoyment.

Chapter Four

The hearing impaired child and the library

THERE ARE DIFFERENT KINDS of deafness producing degrees of hearing impairment. In testing for the degree, an audiometer, measuring in decibels, records on an audiogram chart the hearing frequencies, between 250 Hz and 8,000 Hz, Hz referring to cycles per second. For example, the range can be compared with middle C on the piano, 256 Hz, while the C an octave above is 512 Hz. The ear has a hearing range normally between 50 Hz and 20,000 Hz, while the voice is about two octaves in range.

Hearing impairment can be in the high frequency range, which means that the ear does not hear the consonants, as they are softer when spoken than the vowel sounds. Although hearing aids are carefully tailored to fit a particular wearer's needs, amplification either by raising the voice, or by hearing aid, may not help, as *every* sound is amplified.

For those who were born deaf or who became deaf before learning to speak – the pre-lingually deaf – the difficulties in understanding and communicating are very great. With no model of heard language to aid him, the child has difficulty in speaking and in understanding the spoken word and may therefore become educationally retarded despite normal intelligence.

The child who has partial hearing or who has been deafened later in life, will have heard spoken language and has, therefore, some experience of speech on which to model his own. Both are likely to have defective speech and limited language, and both are likely to have educational and social problems whatever their intelligence and home environment.

Whether pre-lingually or post-lingually impaired, the deaf child needs all the help available to him in aids to speech, aids to hearing and aids to understanding, for each of these affects reading ability.

There is an oralist school of thought and practice that propounds the belief that the child must be taught to communicate orally and to receive communication orally, but this is giving way to the more liberal and helpful practice of using whatever method of stimulation and aid to communication achieves success in speech and understanding. To this end, electronic aids, finger spelling, signing, lipreading and speech are all intended to aid communication and one, some, or all of these may be right and rewarding for the hearing impaired person.

He may employ finger spelling, where the fingers and use of fingers indicate the letters of the alphabet. I have taught hearing children, who were retarded in reading, the alphabet by this means, whereby interest was stimulated by the combination of voice, vision, tactile and reinforced learning. The deaf child may employ signing, which is based on particular handshapes, position in relation to the body, and motion, i.e. particular movements of the hand or hands, and can convey the equivalent of that meaning which comes via intonation for the hearing person, by the use of facial expression, body movement and gesture in conjunction with signing.

In America, the American Sign Language, ASL or Amerslan, is the norm, while in Britain the Paget-Gormon system is the most commonly used example of the British Sign Language or BSL. Other countries also have their own form, for example, Israel's Sign Language, and the International Sign Language has yet other variations.

In Germany, a special tactile language is in common use. Called Lorming, it involves touching the palm or fingers to indicate particular letters and sounds. A special glove with the positions marked on it, means that sighted, hearing people can communicate with blind, deaf people. The whole question of manual language and its relation to the oralist view, and to language communication in general, is informatively and cogently discussed by Mary Brennan in an evaluation of linguistic principles in deaf education called *Can Deaf Children Acquire Language?*[1]

Another method used for people with severe speech difficulties, who are perhaps unable to read or write or have poor hand functioning, is the Bliss Symbol Communication System,[2] which is being taught in some schools. The advantages of the symbols are that they can be read by the able and the handicapped; they are reproduced in chart form and are therefore reasonably portable and economical in terms of money and space. They have a basis in known visual information such as ┌─┐ for table, ↑ for up, with a pattern of symbols for actions and abstracts and for building into sentences. There are, of course, optimum conditions under which the system is feasible and useful, but children with a wide variety of handicaps are said to have benefited. Used by pointing to the appropriate symbol by hand, or in the case of poor hand functioning, by electronic aid, the system has provided some children with the means of talking and reading.

A recent Bliss invention is the portable communication unit, which offers a visual display of symbols, subject-machine interface and an optional speech synthesizer (linked to a computer). It is suggested by the Information Science Section of the Division of Electrical Engineering of the National Research Council of Canada, where the unit was developed, that amongst its many uses the unit's devices can provide non-verbal children with a 'voice'.

The hearing impaired child may have acquired the difficult skill of lipreading. Deaf people and their hearing acquaintances can give many amusing, embarrassing or sad examples of misunderstanding caused by faulty lipreading, but the hearing person needs only to turn off the sound while watching a television programme to gain some idea of the problem of *seeing* the spoken word rather than hearing it. Letters like b, m, p, look alike when the lips form them so that words like 'bad', 'mad', 'baby' and 'paper' look alike when spoken. But worse still, are the sounds not seen on the lips, d,g,k,s,t. Unless the deaf child has some idea of the subject of conversation or aspect of the subject lesson in school, much information is missed or misunderstood.

Total communication using signing, lipreading and speech is coming into current use after a long period of dissension between oralists and manualists, and Dr McCoy Vernon, in an address given at the British Deaf Association Congress in 1974, noted that the conclusions of a large number of independent research studies could be concisely summarized as follows:

> Total communication improves language skills rather than impairs them . . .
>
> Total communication improves academic performance to the point of doubling gains in reading achievement.
>
> Total communication does not impair speech or speechreading skills . . .
>
> With pre-schoolers total communication produced lasting gains in language and educational achievement. By contrast deaf children who had extensive oral pre-school training obtained no lasting benefits.
>
> When total communication is used with hearing parents its potential for helping deaf children is even greater.[3]

The full tables of the research from which this summary came, provide interesting details.

Dr David Denton, the Director of the Maryland School for the Deaf, shows the communication Keystone for total communication in diagrammatic form (see Table 1).

TABLE 1 *Hierarchy of Communication for the Congenitally Deaf Child.*[4]

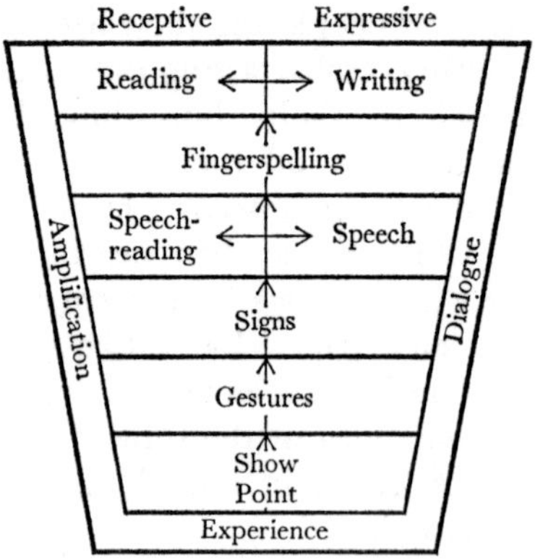

In some countries television programmes for the deaf employ simultaneous forms of communication. In Britain a regular series, *Vision On*, uses visuals, the spoken word, signing, finger spelling, music and sound effects. Similarly in America, Deaf Media Inc. produced a television series called *Rainbow's End*.

The advent of teletext, using computer assisted print on the television screen, ensures that in Britain CEEFAX brings the news and some recorded programmes into the world of the deaf, thus widening the methods and opportunities for the deaf to 'hear'.

Aids to hearing for the deaf child, whether in conversation, teaching or in storytelling, involve the need for awareness of some basic factors on the part of those speaking to the child. It is essential to face the child all the time, but it is part of normal communication to turn the head or body, perhaps to point to something or to bring another person into the conversation, to glance at something that has distracted attention, or to be doing something else while talking.

All these can cause the hearing impaired listener or lipreader to lose many words while the speaker's face and mouth are out of vision. I recently attended a meeting at which a bearded gentleman in the audience asked the hearing speaker at question time what he could do to help deaf children. The speaker said, in a kindly manner, 'Shave off your beard.' Certainly, obscuring the lips by beard, moustache or hands defeats the child who desperately needs every visual clue to understanding speech. As Freddy Bloom says in her picture book, *The Boy who Couldn't Hear*,[5] 'He really hears with his eyes.'

Another physical aid lies in speaking slowly and distinctly. It is not always helpful to speak more loudly, depending on the kind of hearing impairment, nor to mouth in an exaggerated way. Some deaf people can 'hear' better via the vibrations of the speaker's speech, so that a normal pitch and rhythm of speech is useful.

In a paper presented to the 25th Anniversary meeting of the World Federation of the Deaf, in Rome in October 1976, Dr Merrill of Gallaudet College, Washington, discussed the difficulties of striving to support the independence of handicapped people. He asked:

> How does the professional provide a truly helping relationship to the deaf person and at the same time respect his rights as an

> individual? How does the professional, who is prepared to render service to the deaf person in a particular role, such as teaching or counselling, react when he knows that a deaf person is not receiving programmes or services which are equal to those provided for a non-handicapped person? How does the professional become a positive influence in eliminating discrimination against handicapped people by the general public and why should he try to do so?[6]

He notes signs of second-class citizenship, lack of equal access to information, lack of inclusion in public events, lack of sensitivity to deaf people, exclusion from professional roles, lack of influence on policy development, lack of opportunity for self-determination, and suggests the need for new standards of professionalism, consumer representation, professional collegiality, and non-participation in meetings and activities if they reflect an attitude of second-class citizenship for the deaf.

In terms of the content of speech, one of the most difficult tasks of the hearing speaker is to phrase his words in such a way as to exclude unnecessary detail, complicated sentence structure and multiplicity of thoughts. This does not mean that the deaf child should be spoken to using only verbs and nouns, proper sentence structure is important, but the hearing speaker has only to really listen to himself in conversation with other hearing people to realize how many extraneous, duplicated, socially conventional, 'visual' words are used, how often certain things are left unsaid because the meaning was implied in word or sound, and how many times the subject of conversation switches suddenly to a totally different one.

The deaf child benefits from being told the subject, benefits from simple sentences with a single concept, from visual clues from the hands, facial expression or object, from clear speech, and from writing down a word or phrase if there is real difficulty. I was chairing a talk by a profoundly deaf speaker, in which, in the subsequent question time, all questions had to be relayed from the audience via me as the distance from speaker to audience was too great for lipreading. One question involved the subject of book purchase and the question of 'discount' on books for the deaf. The word discount defeated the speaker's lipreading even after I rephrased the question. Relief and understanding, and an answer, came when I wrote down the word discount. Writing words may not seem of help to the deaf child who has not learned to read or who has difficulty, but as an aid to comprehension and to recognizing that word later in printed books, it is a method worthy of consideration.

From the printed word to the electronically-aided word and picture is not a big step in terms of concept or use, but applied to use by the deaf is a gigantic step in terms of speed and ease of comprehension. The invention and mass production of equipment like communicators, microprocessors or word processors, phonetype teleprinters, videotape, teletext, computers and reading machines, to say nothing of the increasing sophistication of hearing aids, mean that sound, vision, and touch, separately or combined, are electronically available as another means of communication for the deaf person. These are described later, in the section on planning and equipment.

The use of drama is a major vehicle of communication denied the hearing impaired child, but in Britain the British Theatre of the Deaf, using mime, speech and signing, brings pleasure and comprehension to many, as does the National Theater of the Deaf in the USA.

The uses of finger spelling, signing, lipreading, speech, drama, electronic or other educational aids, are valuable methods of facilitating communication and acquiring knowledge, but one of the most important aspects of communication with the hearing impaired child is to give him attention, and this is difficult in a group, whether he is in a hearing or hearing impaired group. About 55 per cent of deaf children are educated in ordinary schools and may suffer in this way. The regular visits of the specialist peripatetic or itinerant teacher cover the specialist hearing and learning aspects, but in the course of daily communication the deaf child who needs face to face attention for basic comprehension, often fails to get it when a teacher has a whole class to cater for.

To aid teachers in the regular school where hearing impaired children are in the normal class, the National College of Teachers of the Deaf prepared a booklet, *The Hearing Impaired Child in Your Class*,[7] outlining the ways in which such a child could be helped at nursery, junior and high school levels. It details the limitations imposed by a hearing loss, and provides some tips to ease lipreading problems, and information on hearing aids, teaching and class or group difficulties, and social aspects. That all these need to be described and advised upon, indicates a danger inherent in a policy of mainstreaming without adequate training of the mainstreamed school staff and without resources adequate to class size, space and equipment.

Michael Dininger, co-ordinator of a programme at Gallaudet College, Washington, that watches over nationwide implementation of PL 94–142, the law on the mainstreaming of handicapped children, said:

> Without a high degree of specialized support, the child with a profound hearing loss is not going to be able to do well in a mainstream school. There are many children with a moderate hearing loss who could, with some help, do well ... but what we're seeing around the country is a feeling that the law requires all deaf children to be put into the so-called mainstream. This is a misunderstanding of the law. It's our position that mainstreaming is not going to help a lot of kids who could do better in specialized schools.[8]

A sample of 95 per cent of deaf students aged sixteen plus in America[9] showed that 30 per cent were functionally illiterate, 60 per cent were of grade 5 level or below and 5 per cent achieved a 10th grade or better. In a sample of seventy-three school programmes for deaf children, representing 54 per cent of deaf children aged ten to sixteen, the average reading achievement of a sixteen-year-old was grade level 3 to 4 and the average gain in reading from ages ten to sixteen was less than a year. These findings correspond to those for British children, grade 3 to 4 being the equivalent of the British reading age eight to nine.

This has an obvious effect on the number of deaf children able to go on to college and university. England has only one residential school for the academically able deaf child, the Mary Hare Grammar School in Berkshire, and the percentage of children with that level of ability is similar to that in America.

In Britain there are about eighty schools, primary and secondary, day and boarding, specifically for hearing impaired children; about four hundred units offering tutorial or integrated education; about four hundred peripatetic or itinerant teachers of the deaf attached to most of the local education authorities, but only about fifteen further education centres, for students over sixteen who have left school, which offer courses specifically for deaf students.

Deaf children in Britain begin school at two years of age where possible, simply in order to make a start on the difficult acquisition of language and communication skills without which education, social contacts and general knowledge are unobtainable, and the miscellaneous information that the hearing person picks up is denied the deaf person. The frustrations caused can lead to emotional and behavioural problems which themselves are likely to need some special attention, and all the effects of hearing impairment commonly cause reading retardation to such an extent that the Royal National Institute for the Deaf set up a national literacy scheme to try to improve the 90 per cent illiteracy it estimated in the 25,000 people born severely deaf each year. Even with the literacy scheme, it indicated that 40 per cent would not have sufficient language ability to be able to read books normal to the average seven-year-old.

The severely deaf and those with additional handicaps (most commonly visual, heart, emotional or social) need specialist education and care. Even the child with the single handicap of deafness needs to ensure special attention to his vision. At a deaf school in the Hook of Holland, great emphasis is placed on ensuring that the child's eyesight is corrected, if defective, in order to facilitate lipreading. About 40 per cent of the children need to wear spectacles.

Whether the hearing impaired child is in a special school or unit, is mainstreamed, or at home, he will benefit from co-ordinated policy and action on the part of the education authority. Such a policy is not always the case nationally or locally, in many countries.

Sheffield in Yorkshire, England, has a co-ordinated policy and programme for the children in its area. Based at the Maud Maxfield School for the Deaf, the system involves a co-ordinator who liaises with the headteachers of the ordinary schools in which there are about eighty of the partially hearing children and where there are about three hundred children who wear hearing aids.

The Maud Maxfield School caters for one hundred severely/profoundly deaf children aged three to sixteen of whom over twenty are five-day boarders; and has, in addition to its complement of teachers, a group of peripatetic teachers who visit the hearing impaired children in their ordinary/special schools, or in their homes, to both tutor the child and advise the parents. The Audiology Clinic attached to the education service, carries out much of the diagnostic and assessment work involved in placing the child in the school appropriate to his disability.

However, in many countries, including Britain and America, the quantity and level of help given to the deaf child depends on where he lives, there being variations between one authority and another. Not every education authority has or needs a special school in terms of numbers of learning impaired children resident within its boundaries, but many authorities have shown no support in policy or practice for mainstreaming, or for financing residential care or boarding school places elsewhere for the deaf child needing it.

Further education opportunities for the deaf student vary from country to country. In Italy and America there *is* national recognition of the need for a co-ordinated policy of education from early schooling to further and vocational education. In the USSR deaf students have the right to an interpreter and at one college of eight hundred students there are fifty interpreters. The same interpreter accompanies the same group of students at all times so that the style and continuity of interpreting is maintained. Students and interpreters use total communication.

In most countries where special schooling is available, there is little national co-ordination and few opportunities locally for continuing education in either academic or vocational studies.

Equally, library services are not co-ordinated and librarians are not familiar with the deaf child's library needs. Library needs imply reading skills and the importance of reading skills in library use can be seen in the multiplicity of requirements to read notices, letters, magazines, books, information sheets, and technical instructions.

Reading skill depends not only on the ability to decode the print, but on comprehension of the meaning of words and the deaf child has either not heard words or has not heard as many words as his hearing friend. The deaf child has probably been spoken to in a simplified sentence pattern, in a special, concentrated, deliberate effort to communicate, and has therefore missed the more normal flow of chatter and the background sounds which supply auditory information unconsciously to the hearing person. So the written word is probably the most complete medium of language that the deaf child receives.

In one sense that makes it more difficult, as it presents possibly unfamiliar words and patterns, in another sense it provides him with a means of improving his vocabulary and his knowledge. Some books attempt to find a way round this difficulty by providing a halfway house (itself a term likely to perplex the deaf person) via texts adapted to cater for the experiences and abilities of the hearing impaired person. Examples of texts for class use and books for home reading are given later in this chapter, but one voluntary organization has spent many years adapting 'normal' books for children in order to meet the need for simpler content in terms of sentence patterns and vocabulary, but retaining the original illustrations.

John Wheeler, a teacher for twenty-eight years at the Hamilton Lodge School for the Severely Deaf, in Brighton, of children aged eight to twelve, himself became profoundly deaf at the age of nine after having meningitis. He was the creator of the idea of adapting ordinary children's books, with the permission of the publishers. This involved simplifying the language to cater for the needs of the deaf child, printing the new text on to labels that could be pasted over the normal text and supplying the adapted books to schools and homes, all on a voluntary basis, with a grant for overall expenses from the Breakthrough Trust. These 'easier' versions were given the initial title of the Home Library for Deaf Children.

The project developed slowly until 1977, when Mr Wheeler undertook a market research and publicity drive, contacted publishers whom he hoped would produce the specially adapted versions commercially and, in the light of increasing recognition that such editions had a value for children with other handicaps, changed the project's title to Home Library: simple language editions of books for children. The market research findings can be seen in Appendix 3 and a number of British publishers have expressed interest. The basic list of simple editions, which are sold at the same price as the original limpback editions, includes long standing favourites such as Dick Bruna's books, the *Topsy and Tim* books, *Ameliaranne*, *Giant Alexander* and the *Wombles* books.

Surprisingly, in the same way that the teaching of deaf children provokes conflicting opinions that are typified by the manual or oral teaching methods, so there is a school of thought which is opposed to 'simple' editions on the grounds that the deaf child must learn to cope with normal sentences, concepts, vocabulary and resources. This seems to be a limited view which overlooks the fact that normal book resources *are* available and may be used, and are used by some hearing impaired and other reading retarded children. John Wheeler, in correspondence with me, has said that:

> The opposers of simplified books for deaf children have the whole wide market of children's books available and if they can teach deaf children to read with them that is fine. However they are also supporting the continuation of a situation that has been extant since Caxton (i.e. no books for deaf children). The standard of reading that deaf children attain cannot be called a success story for the 'opposers' views considering that they have had things all their own way. Home Library type books for deaf children *still* not learning to read normal ones cannot be harmful.

The Schools Council Project, Language Development for Deaf Pupils, researched at the University of Sussex, reported that

> Recent research findings in this country have indicated that deaf children using normal reading books and teaching methods make little progress in learning to read; only 40 per cent of them achieve a reading age of 8 by the time they leave school. Such evidence has sometimes led to the production of simplified texts *though these may restrict still further* (my italics) the possibility of the child's advance towards normal reading.[10]

As there is so much evidence, both researched and experiential, that normal books are not particularly helpful either in the teaching of reading, or later in the enjoyment of leisure reading, it is strange that without evidence the Schools Council researchers condemn simplified books, and then, as part of their Project, produce what are, in effect, specially prepared simple booklets and teaching materials. It is neither logical nor humane to object to the simplification of books that are enjoyed by able readers for leisure reading, if such simplification can produce in the hearing impaired child, pleasure, a sense of achievement in having read a book, and the very important feeling of identification with the hearing child who knows about Miffy or Ameliaranne. Later, the simplified editions of books for older children, including the classics and well-known stories, can give the less able reader at least a taste of a story that he will never be able to read in the normal edition. Those who can read the normal editions may do so, and if they wish to read the simpler editions also, why not? We all read below our mental and reading capacity at times, whether in a novel, a magazine or an information book, and gain pleasure in the swift fluency and quick comprehension that this brings.

In Le Raincy in France, the Club des Bibliophiles Handicapés has several objectives, including encouraging access to libraries and book borrowing, promoting concern in the book trade for the needs of the handicapped, and enabling the handicapped to play as full a part in society as possible. The Club was approached by a French deaf children's parents' association which had been looking for adapted books for their children, having seen their frustration and inability to cope with ordinary books. The Club contacted me for advice and I passed on information on the practical, legal and reading aspects and supported the parents' belief in the benefits of adapted books.

The Librarian of the Royal National Institute for the Deaf has mentioned the dearth of British books written for the deaf, and the fact that most teachers of the deaf use whatever ordinary books fill the need. Other workers with handicapped children also seek out the books that can be used, for instance speech therapists.

Many deaf children have speech defects and they, with other children who are speech handicapped by mental, physical or emotional disabilities, may require speech therapy.

A German speech trainer, Gisela Freytag of Munich, uses picture books to support her therapy with such children.[11] She divides the books into five categories:

1 Those that provide one individual picture to a page, to animate and promote inner speech. She uses these for intensive explanation and repetition of the word describing the

object in the picture; for releasing a chain of memories which is transformed into speech; for restoring memory in children who have been unconscious.

2 Those that show a progression of action, which she uses for first sentence patterns.

3 Narrative picture books, which enable the speech trainer to proceed from a single object to actions related to that object and then to other objects and actions. This trains the child towards new words, to focus on a particular object and to react to this.

4 Picture books without words, which stimulate the child to use his own words.

5 Comic strips, which enable the child to see sequence and stimulate him to to recount the story in sentences.

This use of picture books for speech therapy is confirmed by my own experience of using picture books with similar effect and benefit with educationally retarded twelve- and thirteen-year-old boys and girls, and with emotionally disturbed children. I have described this in the section on the librarian and the handicapped child in school and would support the belief that picture books are therapeutic and enjoyable for children over the whole range of handicap. Similarly, Joseph R. Piccolino, Director of the International Media Center at St. Mary's School for the Deaf, in Buffalo, New York, uses pictures and picture books for visual literacy, making pictures function as language.

The provision of books and related materials through library services in school is similar to that for the hearing child, but with emphasis on provision of materials for the less able reader. Patricia Blair Corey suggests in her book, *School Library Services for Deaf Children*,[12] that a nursery school programme of book and library use is necessary to give the deaf child an early start on the long journey to reading skill, and that picture books, though expensive, are needed in greater quantity than for the hearing child, and for a longer period.

Intensive use should be made of visual materials in library lessons and storytime, perhaps having a blackboard, whiteboard or overhead projector on which to write key words and illustrations. The provision of adapted books for deaf children is also common to many school libraries and increasingly to public libraries' children's departments. Three major categories exist in Britain:

1 Some books are adapted by writers as commercially produced editions, often intended for less able hearing children and foreign students learning English and vary from simplified classics to 'remedialized' editions of information books, for example:

Pictorial Classics	Oxford University Press
Kennet Library Modern (popular stories)	Blackie
Phoenix Library (classics)	Blackie
Bullseye Books (adaptations of bestsellers)	Hutchinson Educational
Structural Readers (popular titles)	Longman
Simplified English (2,000 word vocabulary)	Longman
Bridge series (3,000 word vocabulary)	Longman
Heinemann Guided Readers (includes non-fiction also)	Heinemann

Macdonald Easy Reading editions e.g. Introduction to Nature series, Visual series, Countries series.

In Norway one publisher, H. Aschehoug, has produced a number of books for young children, where above the simple text and pictures there are neat drawings illustrating the manual signs. These show the shape of the mouth when speaking the word and the manual sign for each word. An example can be seen in Figure 1.

As a British teacher of the deaf remarked, 'There may be deaf children in England, able to read these Norwegian books better than the English ones.' Though these books are prepared with deaf children in mind, they are marketed through normal channels where they achieve considerable sales, thus normal children benefit also in understanding. As already indicated, there are those who do not approve of the manual methods of communication but the use of manual signs in these books probably makes the difference between partial and total comprehension, and certainly the difference between hard work in

Figure 1

Reproduced from *Thomas Hos Doktoren* by Gunille Wolde, with deaf signs by Mette Newth (H. Aschehoug and Company, Oslo) by courtesy of author and publisher.

reading and enjoyment at the successful achievement of reading a book. Few hearing people would continue to read as a leisure pursuit if it was such hard work, with so many and such frequent perplexities, and uncertainties about comprehension.

2 This category is typified by the adaptations of the Breakthrough Trust, as indicated earlier in the chapter, and these are at present picture books for young hearing children in which the original illustrations remain, but the text is adapted to the kind of word and sentence structure needed for the young deaf child, for example:

Miss Maypole lifted her to the top of the ladder. Janet felt scared as she looked down the long slippery slope. She held on tight to the top of the slide. 'Let go! Let go, Janet!' called Topsy and Tim.	Miss Maypole lifted Janet on to the slide. The children said, 'Come on, Janet'.

Janet let go. SWOOSH she went down the big slide.	Janet went down the slide. She laughed, 'I like this.' Janet was happy.

This is taken from an adaptation by the Home Library for the Deaf, of Jean and Gareth Adamson's *Topsy and Tim at School*.[13] The adapted text fits the visual information supplied by the illustrations, thus aiding comprehension, as in the adaptation of Dick Bruna's *Miffy*.

3 Books and documents adapted or created by teachers to fill the known need in the individual school. Some of the Ladybird books have been adapted by the British Association of Teachers of the Deaf, for example *Scott of the Antarctic*.

To these three categories can be added the many series for teenagers who are less able readers, as listed in the chapter on book selection.

Reference books with clear pictures and unequivocal text are provided, though encyclopaedias are likely to be used much later than with the hearing child. There are learning kits, games, sign language, playing cards, jigsaws and other enjoyable learning and leisure materials that librarians can add to stock.

The hearing impaired child with a chronologically average or near average reading age, has the usual stock of children's books at his disposal in the school or public library, but such children are in the minority.

The library at the Hamilton Lodge School for the Severely Deaf with pupils aged eight to twelve, has about 2,500 books of which four hundred are adapted titles, the rest being carefully selected to cater for the abilities and needs of the children. At the top end of the age range, Gallaudet College in Washington was designed to compensate for hearing loss by giving the students tactile and visual things and there is much use of video for teaching. The high success rate is the result of the individualized instruction system and the library there caters for individual use also, with a vast array of multi-media materials and equipment.

But the hearing impaired child in the regular school or in the public library may miss out on these things if librarians are not aware of the need to emphasize the 'easier' material and the need to individualize the help. Attention to detail for the one or the few deaf children amongst the hearing, makes the difference between a motivated-to-read disadvantaged child and a child further disadvantaged by the inability of the librarian to cater for his special need.

The installation of a hearing-aid loop system in the public library for class or individual visits, is a basic requirement and very necessary if hearing handicapped children share a storytime with hearing children.

The Lansing Public Library in America started a monthly visit for children from the local deaf school, during which conversation and stories were enjoyed and books borrowed. The children, aged seven to eleven, were responsive to stories chosen for their relevance to the children's experience and for the humour. As it is difficult to hold a book and to sign at the same time, the librarian, Joanne Jensen, read the stories while the accompanying teachers signed. Transport problems caused the school to curtail the visits so the librarian took the books to the school for storytime.[14]

In addition to such group activity, individual attention to reading with the child is necessary. Though the deaf child in the library may prefer to be left to read by himself, some do need help. Librarians, like teachers, are usually too busy to read with the individual child in the library and one English teacher of the deaf feels that in both school and public library, there could be a system of volunteers, parents, older students, people in the community, who could 'read-sit' with the children for half an hour daily.

I have already mentioned the benefits of this kind of one-to-one contact between 'helper' and child and book, but the same teacher warned also that some children offer resistance to help from their own parents in one-to-one reading, if they have not done this from the beginning. Thus, guidance to the parents of deaf children, right from the diagnosis of hearing impairment, should include the advice to read *with* the child from babyhood onwards, and librarians in contact with clinics, pre-school groups and kindergartens, need to talk about and provide both the guidance and the appropriate books.

The librarian also needs to be aware of the allowances that must be made for some deaf children in terms of noise and behaviour. When children with hearing impairment speak they may not be able to modulate the voice to fit the circumstances, or their speech may be difficult to follow, requiring more prolonged communication than with a normal library transaction. The deaf child may be unaware that he is making noises, either with his voice or in some other way, including footsteps, banging of doors, slapping of books on the tables and handling of other library items.

He may also be hyperactive or otherwise prone to apparently anti-social behaviour, usually born of continual frustration. Even the children's librarians whose libraries are a hive of activity, emitting a pleasant hum of controlled noise, may be disturbed by the unavoidable and often unconscious noises from some deaf children. In libraries where silence is thought to be necessary, such an apparent breach may call forth a reaction from the librarian which will cause the child to shun the library for ever. So, apart from sustained disruption or deliberate offences, the librarian and other library users should be aware of and make allowances for the possibility of unusual noise in the library.

The need for audio-visual equipment in the library is self evident when its use in the classroom is so common. To be shut off from such communication in the library for lack of equipment makes a mockery of the principle that public libraries are open to all and the information in them freely available. Similarly in the ordinary school library.

The freedom to learn by self-educating methods which are open to those who can read, see and hear, may be denied the deaf and blind if *their* self-educating hardware and software are not available.

The librarian in a school or public library serving deaf children will provide a better service both in materials and in understanding, if he or she knows the language of the deaf and has information concerning the local school curriculum and the reading problems of the hearing impaired. Thus, self-education into the world of the deaf is part of the librarian's task in providing an effective library service.

A library's purpose for being is to facilitate communication through print and non-print sources and any aid it can give to facilitating communication for the handicapped, complements and supplements the work of those who begin, against great odds, the long task for both teacher and child, of sharing thoughts via words.

Virginia Guldager of the Perkins School for the Blind in Massachusetts, describes this process in a paper on communication and the multiply handicapped child, the deaf-blind or rubella child.

> Rubella children have had pre-natal damage . . . they are often visually and aurally handicapped. They have heart defects, liver and spleen defects, extensive damage to the central nervous system, are often microcephalic, have defective teeth, severe feeding problems and may be subject to frequent infections. The children who present special educational problems are those with a combination of several of these congenital defects.

In order to learn to communicate the child must imitate, but in order to imitate the child must somehow see, hear and feel the other and copy what is seen, heard and felt, which is not easy for a child with multiple handicaps.

> Perhaps he can imitate the positions of a doll and then a photograph and then a drawing and then a stick figure. Perhaps he can imitate a simple story in picture form . . . perhaps presenting the stick figure with the spoken word and the written word he can learn to read and understand single words or simple sentences. Perhaps by imitating speech movements and sounds, he can learn to speak and attach meaning to words as his experiences are systematically accumulated.[15]

While this is a long task for both teacher and child, the potential outcome is improved communication, and while that is one of the objectives of all education and all libraries, it is particularly crucial for the hearing and speech impaired child, whose mental faculties are often unimpaired and who therefore suffers frustration because of the obstacles he encounters in his contact with books, libraries and librarians.

Chapter Five

The visually handicapped child and the library

THE WORLD HEALTH ORGANIZATION estimates that there are, each year, 100,000 pre-school children in the developing world who are blinded by a vitamin deficiency disease, such nutritional blindness being common in India, Indonesia, Haiti, the Philippines and Bangladesh.[1]

An estimated 20 to 40 million people in Africa suffer from river blindness and about 500 million people in many countries are blinded by Trachoma, a chronic infection caused by intracellular parasites, a result of overcrowding and insanitary habits. All this is preventable, but only by a campaign to improve health, diet and living standards.

In the 'developed' world visual handicaps arise from other causes, but the result is the same. The American Foundation for the Blind estimates that 6·4 million visually handicapped live in America, 1·7 million of these being severely affected. The National Society for the Prevention of Blindness estimates that one out of every 500 school age children is visually impaired and there are about 35,000 legally blind children, of whom about 5,000 are deaf-blind, often the result of rubella during pregnancy.

In the United Kingdom there are about 100,000 registered blind of whom about 4,000 are visually handicapped children. So although numbers are smaller than for some other handicaps, the number could be further reduced by better health and social care, and preventive medicine.

The category of legal blindness is, internationally, usually defined as a person with 20/200 vision, that is, he can see at 20 feet what a sighted person can see at 200 feet. But within this there are numerous variations and conditions which cause a person to see more or less than that, ranging from the near-blind to vision that can be corrected by the use of spectacles. Most legally blind people are not in fact totally sightless, but have partial sight with varying degrees of usefulness. However, all sources warn that partial sight and dual and multiple handicaps are increasing, thus, though work is progressing on identifying causes and alleviating conditions, the existing handicapped children must be cared for and preparations made for catering for the increasing numbers.

In many countries the severely visually handicapped child is likely to attend a residential school, particularly if he has other handicaps too. Some partially sighted children also need this kind of care. Other children attend special day schools, or units in ordinary schools, or are in ordinary schools where help is given when it is needed.

In Britain, educational provision may be in residential schools for the full age range or, as in the case of the Tapton Mount School in Sheffield, for ages five to twelve, where the 'open education' scheme means that selected visually handicapped children can then attend the local comprehensive school for sighted children, while living in a hostel on the residential school campus.

In Harrogate, the Henshaw School for the Visually Handicapped caters for about eighty residents aged twelve to eighteen. The students have varying kinds of visual disability which require special help and some have a physical impairment also. About one-third are educationally two or three years behind their sighted contemporaries. The prominence given to the library there, is indicative of the staff's attitudes towards books and reading.

The library is visually very attractive with shelving well spaced to allow for easy movement between the stacks; the large tables are necessary to cater for the large size of many braille volumes and kits, and the extra amount of personal space required by visually impaired people. There are collections of teaching materials in each classroom, but the central library offers around 1,000 braille volumes, most of the available large print books for children and adults, normal print hardback and paperback books, braille and large print reference books, and music scores. There are some braille periodicals, *Argosy*, *Braille*

Sporting Record Weekly, *Trend*, *Home Help*, *Trefoil Trail*, *Fleur de Lys*, *Jack and Jill* and the *Braille Library Bulletin*. The boys particularly enjoy *Sporting Record Weekly*.

When I visited the library the school's headmaster commented on the fact that blind children are often very verbal, since proven to me time and again, and the articulacy of the young people with regard to their reading likes and dislikes was notable. Just like their sighted peer group they like Enid Blyton and the Hardy Boys, and they like to follow their personal hobbies by reading about them. But they feel very isolated from teenage sighted friends because there is little access to the pop-world gossip and the comic strip characters or, for the girls, the personal grooming information in women's magazines or, the boys said, the sex aspects in books and magazines. The braille edition of *Penthouse* was not on the market then, as it is now, and would be unlikely to be subscribed to by a school anyway. Even an American university has been attacked for subscribing to it.

The dearth of braille non-fiction and reference books in large print was also a complaint from the Henshaw students, who knew of the enormous range of non-fiction for the sighted reader. Such a lack may well be overcome now that computers linked to braille printers mean speedier transcription. But all the students were keen users of what was available and felt envious of the information media available for the sighted reader.

Partially sighted children may be in ordinary schools, integrated with special help, or in units for the partially sighted attached to ordinary schools. There is strong evidence that sight defects go undetected in many children in ordinary primary schools until it is noticed that the child is not keeping up with his class.

The special help needed may include special equipment for learning and reading, possibly mobility training, and probably extra help because of educational retardation. New inventions are frequent, many of them originating or being tested at the Perkins School for the Blind in Massachusetts, USA.

This school epitomizes the work, and the ambience of the work, of preparing the visually handicapped for participation in life, for it is notable for its successful education and training over many years, for its most famous student Helen Keller whose centenary it is in 1980, and for what is probably the largest collection in the world of print and research materials catering for its pupils, its research programmes, its in-service training courses and its role as a Regional Center for the Library of Congress service to the blind and physically handicapped.

The students have varying kinds of visual handicap, and, in some cases, have accompanying handicaps, such as deafness, mental retardation, moderate emotional problems, or perceptual dysfunction, and the library reflects this range.

The students are provided with a wide range of knowledge and special skills through an educational programme covering academic subjects, music, arts and crafts, industrial arts, vocational training, including piano tuning and repair, and commercial subjects, physical education, home economics and management, mobility, daily living skills, various therapies, and recreational and social experiences and skills.

With the 1975 legislation requiring mainstreaming where possible, it was necessary to ensure that the Perkins School offered courses and skills which the ordinary schools could not. In addition to such courses, a summer vacation programme is run for those visually handicapped children in regular schools who need the special aspects not provided in those schools.

About one-third of the students are deaf-blind and most students use sign language to communicate. The school administers courses in signing for adults, in order to teach those who work with the deaf-blind child, teachers, parents, child care personnel, administrative and maintenance staff, friends, volunteer interpreters and others. To help such adult students the *Perkins Sign Language Dictionary* was published in 1975, containing 2,200 sign descriptions, of which about 85 were invented to meet the vocabulary needs of students in careers, home management and pre-vocational work programmes. Other signing texts are produced at, and are available from, Gallaudet College, Washington. For instance, pre-school signed English programmes in three series, Beginning, Stories and Poems, and Growing Up Books. The college has also produced *Animals in Signs* and *Home in Signs*, both by F. Caccamise and C. Norris, and *Handtalk: an ABC of fingerspelling and sign language*.[2]

The Bliss Symbol Communication System, also a sign language, is predominantly visual and is used most often with physically, hearing and speech impaired children. It is described in the section on the hearing impaired child.

At Perkins, as at all the other schools for the visually handicapped that I have visited, the impression is one of visual attraction which can be described to the blind person, if not actually seen by him. For the children at Perkins the school library contains all the types of material normally required, braille, both hand and press, large print, audio-visual media, twin-vision – a combination of print and braille or print and tactile surfaces – periodicals and ordinary books. The library staff attend meetings of various book selection committees both locally and nationally, for example those of the Children's Science Book Review Committee and of the Library of Congress Children's Book Advisory Council, where books to be brailled and recorded are recommended.

In addition to the library in the school and the Waterton (research) Library, the 'houses' also have collections of material for the students' recreational use. The Perkins Museum is administered by the Research Librarian/Curator and contains all kinds of materials which the catalogue lists under the following headings: rocks and minerals, sea life, plant life, shells, fish, reptiles, amphibians, insects, birds, animals, shoes, geometrical forms, art, skeletal structures, industrial arts, shops, dolls, transportation, Malayan articles, fossils, artefacts, and architecture.

As part of the learning resources of the Perkins School, this collection is important in supplying information by touch and vision which might otherwise be supplied to the sighted child by print or by textbook illustration, and teachers are encouraged to use the items for class lessons.

The use of senses other than sight is well described in an article written by a blind, deaf-dumb person who became thus handicapped after having meningitis at the age of two and a half:

> I knew my schoolmistress by the tobacco smell, her eau-de-Cologne and by her fine hand, medium in size . . . I imagined the persons I came into contact with according to their rough or fine hands . . . fat or lean, long or short fingered. According to their smell I realized if they were smokers or drinkers . . . the kind of work they performed. . . . During our walks into town, we felt

> around us the cars' trepidations and the gasolene smell . . . I touched with my hands different instruments on which our school pupils played. I felt the vibrations and I realized if the matter was of a sprightly or a slow melody . . . I realized that, by systematical training this tactile sense can be developed.[3]

Such sensitivity is also important in the fingertips for braille reading and some children do not have or develop the necessary sensitivity for fluent braille reading.

Braille involves a system of raised dots juxtaposed to produce different letters and combinations of letters, with a further advanced system for words or even sentences. There is also Nemath or braille mathematics and braille music, with sixty-three symbols. Even Opticon, an electronic system, requires fingertip reading, using a 'light pen' which, when passed over printed words, transmits the words to equipment which translates them into a vibrating tactual pattern which can be 'read' by the fingers.

In braille reading the fingers read the dots, but speed depends upon the degree and efficiency of training, the alertness of the mind and the sensitivity of the fingertips. Thus, not all those who need the skill can acquire it. It is estimated that the fast braille reader has a reading speed of about 160 words a minute but the average is around 100. This equates with a normal reading aloud speed and is about half a sighted reader's speed. The time taken to read large print or to manage ordinary print, is greater than for the sighted reader, and when to the visual handicap is added the possibility of a 'slow learner' state, there is further retardation of reading speed and of comprehension. Another scheme, Moon, invented by William Moon of Brighton, is in use, often by the elderly or the digitally insensitive. Here the raised aspects are letters rather than dots. The National Library for the Blind in Britain, offers about eight hundred titles in Moon for loan, these are mostly adult titles.

Just as there is a need for simple books for the sighted reader with reading difficulty, so such a need exists for the braille and large print reader. Some simple reading series have been converted into braille, for example, Windrush, Onward, Forward, and Inner Ring series.

But handicapped children have the same reading interests and tastes as non-impaired children. Any difference lies in the stage of development or age at which those needs and interests apply. Thus, the full range of reading matter should be available, in addition to the special need for braille, large print, tapes, recorded material, and the relevant hardware.

The choice of books for reading aloud, either in storytelling or on tape, is from amongst those which contain text strong enough to stand without illustration. But a problem arises for the very young visually handicapped child who cannot yet read braille or print and whose sighted contemporaries are 'reading' picture books. The increasing availability of books with raised outline pictures is a step in the right direction for such children.

An excellent example is *What's That?* by Virginia Allan Jensen and Dorcas Woodbury Haller.[4] Here the children are able to see pictures with their fingers and by a combination of textured shapes and printed text the book can be shared by both sighted and handicapped reader, as a story and as a conversation piece.

Twin Vision is a special publishing house in California, producing thousands of titles in twin editions from Peanuts to the Declaration of Independence, in raised pictures, print and braille in thermoplastic medium.

In a paper presented to a joint meeting of the IFLA Children's Libraries Section and the Hospital and Handicapped Readers Section at Lausanne in 1976, the Director of the Italian Library for the Blind at Monza described some of the work there.

Raised thermoplastic surfaces provide a variety of tactile experiences in, for instance, Kipling's *Elephant's Child.* The book was obtained on thermoplastic sheets, using cardboard patterns of different thicknesses. Where appropriate the patterns were covered by materials simulating crocodile, snake and hippopotamus skins.

Other books with fur, wood or cloth applications are available to aid understanding of objects. Relief maps and atlases are also made for use by the visually handicapped and the idea could be extended to encyclopaedias, the illustration of scientific books and practical manuals. Indeed tactual maps would be useful in mobility training, preferably with interchangeable pieces.

It is clear that where the sighted child might say 'I have seen that animal/tree/cup before,' the visually handicapped child might say, 'I have felt that animal skin/tree/cup before,' and the recognition brings the same pleasure, identification and satisfaction, though the means are different.

The provision of print material raises a number of points. Research has shown that legibility is improved if the following features are present:

1 Increased print size and ample space between the lines (leading pronounced ledding).
2 Extra weight of print, meaning blacker ink and/or thicker strokes.
3 Sans-serif type, which provides an even stroke weight and, in the absence of serifs, does not distract the eye.
4 Non-glare paper, glare being common on many pages of text and illustration. Glare is liable to occur also when many visually handicapped children lay the book flat on the table to facilitate easier viewing.

Increase in the size of print does not necessarily aid reading for all visually handicapped people. Alison Shaw, author of *Print for Partial Sight*, suggests that perhaps 35 per cent may be so helped.[5] She recognizes that partially sighted children have a greater ability to see than adults if the book or object is held close to the eyes. She also acknowledges that factors such as the reader and the content of the reading material are crucial to both comprehension and motivation. There is no doubt, however, that reading large print is less fatiguing visually.

Point size is only an approximate guide, for example 12 point Perpetua (small on the body) looks about 10 point Times (large on the body) and sans-serif faces usually appear large in relation to their point size. Increase in legibility is not enough if comprehension does not follow. The text itself must be suited to the reading level, and chronological and interest levels of the child, and it is estimated that at least one-third of visually handicapped children are retarded in reading.

The criteria for selection of books for such children should be those applied to the reading retarded generally. But for all children who have any degree of vision the provision of illustration is vital, well-defined colour pictures providing not only interest, but information on the theme and clues to the text. The selector needs to pay particular attention to the quality of illustration in terms of legibility, and two examples of select lists of materials suitable in text and illustration are:

1 Marshall, Margaret R. *Seeing Clear: books for the partially sighted child.* Oxford: School Library Association, 1977.
2 Hunsicker, Marya. When the blind begin to read. *School Library Journal*, November 1972, pp. 79–81.

The children's book section of *Large Type Books in Print*, New York: Bowker, 1978, covers about three hundred titles of children's books with print 14 point or larger, and gives grade levels.

Most are ordinary children's books which happen to be in large type and there is no attempt to match the visual legibility of the illustrations.

The importance of colour cannot be overstressed. Apart from its attraction, colour provides information, but however attractive and informative the illustrations are, whether photographs or paintings, the practical legibility occurs in the clear outlines of what is illustrated. Increasing the size of illustration or object illustrated, does not always help with some kinds of visual impairment, as that would require the eye to move over a bigger area before the object could be identified. Clearly defined content is of greater importance than size. Black and white, or even colour photographs may not pass the legibility test if the photographer has not skilfully angled the camera to draw attention to the pertinent aspect, intended to illustrate the point being made.

The normal eye and reader may well be able to perceive the particular detail, both visually and mentally, from a wealth of visual detail, but the visually handicapped child should be aided by pictures which pinpoint the relevant aspects for him. This does not mean that the child does not get pleasure from 'busy' pictures; given time and motivation he will linger over pictures like the sighted child. But whereas the sighted child will glance at the picture accompanying the text to gain a clue to what the text is about, the visually handicapped child will need to make an effort to see, that is, he must *work* at seeing, rather than give the effortless glance.

Effortless glancing at magazines by sighted children and

young people is often taken for granted by them. The advantages of magazines and periodicals lie in the possibility of up-to-date information, condensed or strictly pertinent text and a quantity of visual information in photographs, diagrams and illustrations.

Whether they are concerned with 'serious' educational matters or are of recreational/personal interest, such periodicals are denied to the visually handicapped person except for a small number produced in braille or recorded.

The Division of Libraries for the Blind and Physically Handicapped produced over fifty popular magazines in braille or recorded format, of which about eight brailled magazines and six disc magazines are of interest to children and young people. In addition, some cassette magazines such as *Contemporary Sound Tracks*, *Musical Mainstream* and *Young Adults Magazine on Talking Books*, all bi-monthly, provide personal interest information for the older child and teenager.

In Britain a similar number of braille magazines are suitable for children and young people, while in Italy the Italian Library for the Blind in Monza promotes a free monthly review in braille for children aged eleven to fifteen. Called *Minimondo*, it covers topical questions and provides information on sport, fashion and music.

The library provision of such material aids the wider educational, social and personal growth of the visually handicapped child and enables him to be in touch with the same themes as the sighted child, minus the visual content.

The librarian selecting stock therefore takes account of the variations in content, from the simplest picture books and talking book stories for the young to the adult novel and the 'good' children's books, such as those in the Division for the Blind and Physically Handicapped's production of the American Newbery and Caldecott Awards books on tape and in braille, and the Italian Library for the Blind's Monza Prize, which is an award given annually for a children's book in narrative rather than visual terms, the winner of which is transcribed into braille. He also takes account of the variations in reading ability in whatever medium, and the variations in vision, visual acuity and visual perception.

Certain aspects of librarianship for children need special

attention when serving the visually handicapped child. The American *Standards for Library Services to the Blind and Visually Handicapped*, published in 1967, covered the size and content of library collections, staffing, services, aid and equipment, and physical facilities in the following types of library: federal, state and regional, community, school and agency. In large print, the Standards deal with recommended principles and practices. Taking these as a basis, it is possible to look more closely at their application.

The standard of ten books per child, while it equals that recommended for ordinary schools by both the American and British school library standards, has certain constraints in terms of space, cost and duplication required.

1 The cost of braille books is so much greater than that of conventional books, probably five times the cost, and the wear and tear on the plastic dots and raised surface material means constant replacement and therefore added cost.

The durability of braille depends upon the heavy-handedness of the braille reader. For example, beginners in braille tend to be less adept and the materials used by them need replacing sooner. The use of thermoplastic material for some purposes reduces wear and tear.

The special materials needed are initially more expensive than reading materials for the sighted reader and when the cost of frequent replacement is added, the library budget requirement must be proportionately more than for an ordinary school library. An example of one item will indicate the point; Webster's *New World Dictionary of the American Language*, printed in 18 point, is in twenty-four volumes and in 1978 sold at 399 dollars. In Braille it is in seventy-two volumes, is sold at 1460 dollars and requires sixteen feet of shelf space. In England, the *Little Oxford Dictionary of Current English*, normally a pocket sized dictionary selling at just under £2.00, has been published in large print by Ulverscroft at just under £9.00.

2 The same title may be needed in several formats to cater for the differing visual abilities; in braille, large print, recorded and conventional book form. The same applies to periodicals and newspapers and to the library catalogue, which

may need to be in braille and large print as well as conventional print. Similarly the guiding on the shelves and book spines may need to be in conventional numbers, symbols and words and in braille.

3 The cost of subscriptions to organizations such as the National Library for the Blind and the Royal National Institute for the Blind for the acquisition of special materials, is an extra for the library budget.

4 Space is a priority, since more shelf space is needed, often oversize shelving, for a smaller number of books. Table space is needed for the larger books, for the kits and games, and the space between furniture and shelves must allow for greater freedom of movement than would be needed for sighted children.

5 The extra cost of stationery, postage and brailling of documents is another factor.

6 Equipment needed in the library adds to the expense. The Standards suggest that the following equipment should be available:

(a) At least one standard typewriter.
(b) Optical aids in quantity.
(c) At least one large print typewriter.
(d) At least one braille writer.
(e) At least one tape recorder.
(f) At least one 4 speed record player or talking book machine.
(g) At least one device for duplicating items recorded on magnetic tape.
(h) At least one braille duplicator and binder.

To these can be added the desirability of special reading stands which can be raised, tilted and angled as well as laid flat to facilitate the angle, projection and distance needed for reading by each of the pupils who has to adopt an individual visual angle.

Closed-circuit television, which can magnify print up to forty-five times, has a place in the library as well as in the classroom. Add to this the desirability of a whiteboard and an overhead projector to aid library instruction classes, and the total list indicates an expenditure of money and a provision of space which is unlikely to be available in the average school for the visually handicapped.

The implication of this for the ordinary school into which the visually handicapped child may have been mainstreamed, is that the librarian needs to think and plan for the adequate coverage of necessary items so that the few visually handicapped children do not suffer. It may not be possible to purchase all the items, but within the school, whether special or ordinary, there are usually some of the listed items; whiteboards, overhead projectors, standard typewriters, tape recorders, duplicating for magnetic tape and equipment for film material.

Co-ordinating its use for the visually handicapped can be done by one or more of the following:

1 Housing one of each of the items in the library.
2 Arranging for a personal carrel to be set up within the library with these items as fixtures, for the use of the handicapped child.
3 Liaising with all the teachers who have a visually handicapped child in their classes, to notify the librarian, in advance, of work set which might require the handicapped child to use different materials from his sighted classmate, so that the appropriate materials, software and hardware, can be located, retrieved and supplied, either in the library or wherever local conditions demand. The provision of optical aids or braille equipment is likely to be made either personally by the child, by the national library, the social service or in conjunction with a school for the visually handicapped.

Staffing is recommended by the Standards as one full-time professional librarian for each hundred students after the first 100, and clerical staff as one clerk-typist-braillist for each hundred students. These are recommended as being needed to provide service to the same standard as a sighted school.

The selection and acquisition of appropriate materials, the special cataloguing and processing needed, the maintenance of files of information, possibly the recording of information, liaison with other libraries and agencies nationally and locally; these all have a special application and may require duplicate servicing formats in print and braille.

An important responsibility of anyone staffing a library for the visually handicapped is that of assisting the user to locate both information and materials in that library and via other libraries, and this takes time. There are, of course, discrepancies between the Standards and the practice in special schools in the matter of staff.

At the Henshaw School, a sighted teacher has the library responsibility and a teaching load. She instituted a number of timesaving short cuts, such as recording the loan of an item by clipping the reader's name card to the catalogue card, thus indicating in one record, what books the library has, whether the book is on the shelf or on loan and, if the latter, who has it. In a small school with a teacher spending some of her time on the administration of the library and using the school secretary and the volunteer braillists, it was possible to offer a usable and attractive library service.

Few qualified librarians have specialized in work with the handicapped while at library school, and there are few post-qualification courses, either external or in-service, to which the interested librarian could go. But the bibliographical skills of the trained librarian stand him in good stead in obtaining both specialist information on visual handicap and the information needed by his users.

The Standards stress the importance of bibliographic information and this is increasing in the USA, Britain and the Scandinavian countries. Although the national bibliographies do not distinguish between the materials for special and ordinary categories, special bibliographies are attempting to provide this information.

The Library of Congress Division for the Blind and Physically Handicapped runs a free national library service providing braille and recorded materials. These materials are entered in catalogues and bibliographies such as:

Large Print Scores and Books Catalog
Instructional Disc Recordings Catalog
Instructional Cassette Recordings Catalog
Biennial catalogues such as *For Younger Readers: braille and talking books*

Bi-monthly catalogues such as *Braille Book Review* and *Talking Book Topics*

Subject bibliographies on Science, Sports and Magazines, are available in large print, braille and disc editions.

For Younger Readers covers a two-year period and lists about four hundred books, fiction and non-fiction, in subject groupings, in sections labelled: For Very Young Readers, Young Readers Non-Fiction, Young Readers Fiction, Spanish Titles. Listed alphabetically by title, a plot/content description is given and an age grading.

Animal Fair is a subject bibliography of books for children which have appeared in *Talking Book Topics* and *Braille Book Review*. The annotated list covers animal books in non-fiction – eighteen titles; fiction on talking book record – ninety fiction titles, four non-fiction; thirteen fiction titles on talking book cassettes and twenty-four non-fiction; and fifty-one fiction titles on Press Braille.

Similarly, in Britain the National Library for the Blind provides a listing catalogue of braille children's books, and a list of Austin Books, classic works in large print. The Royal National Institute for the Blind provides catalogues of its Students Braille Library and the Tape Library for Students.

In Australia, talking books are obtained via the Talking Book Library in Melbourne, and the Royal Blind Society in Sydney offers a national service, the Braille and Talking Book Service. The Red Cross also supplies talking books, while in Tasmania a voluntary organization offers the Hear a Book Service. Added to these are the publishers' catalogues and the catalogues of producers of large print and talking books, for example, G. K. Hall, Ulverscroft, Chivers, Magnaprint, Caedmon, Listening Library, Calibre.

Taped books can be obtained at normal reading speed and at slow reading speed, and cassette equipment is available for variable speed adaptation. Whereas a normal book may take twelve or more hours to 'read' on tape, the faster speed adjustment can reduce that by half. It is possible that comprehension increases with increased speed of reading, thus students and slow learners alike may benefit.

The Standards recommend liaison with other libraries and agencies, and this is practised by the great majority of libraries serving the visually handicapped.

Whether a community library, school library or regional library, much of the print and talking book stock will be there on loan from the national library service. In the USA, the Library of Congress Division's service is offered via more than fifty regional and one hundred sub-regional or community libraries, to registered visually and physically disabled people.

In Britain, the postal services from the National Library for the Blind and the Royal National Institute for the Blind enable individuals and institutions to obtain books and audio materials. Such liaison also involves the equipment needed for using the audio-visual software, and the Library of Congress Division supplies headphones, amplifiers to boost headphones, plastic tone arm clips and pillow phones for people confined to bed. In Britain, equipment is available through the Social Services Departments in each local authority.

In Sweden, where state grants cover provision for the blind via public libraries, talking books are loaned and sold by the centralized library agency, Bibliotekstjänst. In several countries talking newspapers are produced, some by public libraries, some by business men's organizations, some by consortia in the community.

Contact with other organizations may be necessary, like the Torch Trust for the Blind; the Optical Information Council, which publishes a pamphlet entitled *So You're Partially Sighted...*; the BBC, which publishes *In Touch: aids and services for the blind*; and the Royal Institute of British Architects (RIBA) which has looked at some of the problems of the blind in its publication, *Designing for the Disabled.* The American Foundation for the Blind produces many publications in addition to the Printing House List.

Many organizations are concerned with one or other aspect of visual handicap and the library needs to keep a file of such contacts, both local and national.

It seems very possible that the handicap of impaired vision can be mitigated, in terms of reading, by the developments of the electronic age. Computer produced text, pictures and voice; computer braille print-out; computer assisted transcription from print to tactual media; tape recording; and the brain implants to produce 'vision' are all in existence, for the few who can afford them or have access to school-owned equipment. But all still require the use of senses other than sight, and most visually handicapped children do not yet have access to the technology.

Thus, visually handicapped children remain largely deprived of the imaginative and informative stimulus of books, until technology, teachers and librarians, and those who finance them all, can provide the material to match the need.

Chapter Six

The physically handicapped child and the library

THE CHILD with a physical handicap is usually a 'normal' child who happens to have a physical disability, though physical handicap is sometimes the result of mental impairment.

In an article in *Link*, the journal of the Association of Spina Bifida and Hydrocephalus, five girls aged fifteen to seventeen, disabled by spina bifida (of whom there are about 1,500 born annually in Britain) wrote of their activities:

> I have already passed my RSA typing and CSE arithmetic . . . my latest venture is learning to drive . . . when I first came to Coney Hill I could hardly stand. Now I have been able to complete a four mile sponsored walk and can manage stairs very well.
>
> I belong to an ordinary Ranger unit. We have been ten-pin bowling. One of my greatest interests is photography.
>
> We are encouraged to make decisions for ourselves and are also encouraged to join outside activities which as well as being good for us is also great fun.
>
> I do fencing and have just won a bronze award for it . . . some of us had a lovely day in France . . . We go to youth meetings at the church . . . we are doing a production of Mikado . . . but it is quite difficult to find suitable costumes for us all.
>
> I can play 4 instruments, the piano, guitar, violin and recorder. I hope to take a violin exam.[1]

Such activities, and enthusiasm for them, would shame many able-bodied teenage girls, but mention of them here is intended only to emphasize the importance of talking and socializing with the average physically handicapped child in the same way as with the average able-bodied child.

The range of physical handicap is enormous, including spina bifida, cerebral palsy, chest and kidney conditions, congenital defects such as heart abnormalities, hydrocephalus and birth injuries, bone conditions, skin and muscular conditions, blood abnormalities and the results of road and other accidents.

The physically handicapped child may be in an ordinary school, a special day school, a residential school, in hospital or at home, with home tuition. Some special schools cater for one type of disability, for example cerebral palsy, spina bifida or asthma; others accommodate a variety of physical disability. In Britain most cover the age range five to sixteen. A number of local education authorities make special nursery schools available for handicapped children and some offer reserved places in further education colleges.

For example, the Hereward College of Further Education in Coventry offers a large number of places to physically handicapped people over sixteen who are of average or above average intelligence. The courses include office and business studies, engineering, and general education. Some residential places are available, and there are nurses and a medical officer in attendance. Many such colleges make no distinction between the able-bodied and the physically handicapped in enrolment terms, but cannot offer the medical or physical facilities to ensure adequate aid if needed.

An example of one school's range of disability is seen at the John Jamieson School for the Physically Handicapped in Leeds. The school serves an area of over half a million inhabitants, of whom 100,000 are children between six and fifteen years. At the time of writing the school had 172 children and the diagnoses were as follows:

48 spina bifida
2 other spinal conditions
48 cerebral palsy
5 others
3 chest conditions
2 kidney conditions
10 congenital heart defects

2 multiple anomalies
6 hydrocephalus
3 birth injuries
4 scoloi – kyphoses
2 fragilitas ossium
6 other bone conditions
3 skin conditions
8 muscular dystrophy
5 other muscular conditions
5 haemophilia
3 other blood conditions
7 road and other accidents

The children leave the school when they are (a) surgically and/or physically fit, (b) too ill or too handicapped to attend, in which case they may qualify for home tuition, (c) educationally and emotionally able to fit into another school, and (d) able to work. Children with any of these handicaps may be educationally and reading retarded, despite their often sophisticated and intelligent minds, because of the continual hospitalization or treatment periods and therapy; the drug régimes; in some cases incontinence and in others continuous pain, all of which affect concentration and reduce the time available for formal learning. With some of the conditions the children will have both greater suffering and a shorter life expectancy, and of those children who do reach adulthood, many will not reap the full benefits thereof, physically, socially or emotionally. Some make remarkable contributions to society, in the family, in the local neighbourhood, and nationally. Generalization about the physically handicapped is as dangerous as with most other handicaps, each person being unique, but an example of one type of handicap may indicate the range of problems encountered in understanding and attempting to remedy the effects of the handicap.

The number of children with spina bifida in British schools for the physically handicapped is about 1,500 and is second only to the number of children with cerebral palsy. Some 800 are educated in ordinary schools and of these about 250 wear appliances for incontinence, about 150 are in wheelchairs and about 120 have a valve to relieve fluid in the head.

The term spina bifida includes a number of types of condition, occulta, cystica, myelomeningocele. There may be complications like hydrocephalus, excessive fluid on the brain, which can also occur, usually as a congenital defect, and eye defects such as squinting, which are related to the condition.

The effects on the child are such that from birth he is likely to need the attention of neuro-surgeons, urologists, orthopaedic surgeons, paediatricians, doctors, nurses, occupational therapists, physiotherapists, social workers, psychologists and teachers.

When the child with spina bifida or the child with cerebral palsy is able to attend an ordinary school, in addition to the continuing care of all these specialists, he is likely to need special tuition. There are variations in intelligence, specific learning difficulties rather than general retardation, such as difficulty in sensory organization, motor ability, spatial and conceptual difficulties.

Where reading is concerned he may be behind the other children, partly because he has missed a lot of schooling due to hospitalization or ill health. His eye defects are likely to retard reading in that he may be unable to scan a page; his spatial disability may make it difficult for him to return to a place on the page if he takes his eyes from it momentarily, and he is often unable to distinguish a figure against a 'busy' background. He is thus unable to learn from many illustrations in the normal way. His visual perception may preclude accurate identification of shapes and letters. His conceptual ability may also be impaired, and as this relates to his total experience it also affects his reading and his comprehension of what is read.

A helpful pamphlet, *Children with Spina Bifida in School: a booklet for teachers and students*,[2] gives advice to the ordinary school teacher on how to help such children, pointing out that the guidelines apply also to other handicaps and children with learning problems, for example:

1 Early identification.
2 Early training.
3 Systematic plan of remediation.
4 Encouraging alternative means of expression.
5 Encouraging the child's own strong points.
6 Maintaining motivation.
7 Preparing strategies for dealing with distractability.

Distractability is very common in children with spina bifida and cerebral palsy, who seem to react to every stimulus from every source, without selectivity, thus the need for systematic reinforcement and reward for attention. Many children within the range of severity in the handicap do learn to read and to read fluently, but the majority remain in need of continuing aid to attain both fluency and comprehesion. The majority of physically handicapped children are not mentally deficient, though they may be educationally behind their age group, and an active mind in a constrained or dysfunctioning body can cause immense frustration, hence the inclusion of the word 'emotionally' in the John Jamieson School's consideration of ability to cope in an ordinary school. Added to the difficulties are those of the developing teenage desire for independence, often a problem in an able-bodied teenager, but beset with further difficulty for the physically handicapped youngster.

In other special schools, often for the delicate child, there may be epileptic and diabetic children who find life difficult in ordinary schools and those children with psychological problems arising from ill health.

Some surveys of children assessed as physically and emotionally able to be integrated into ordinary schools after being in special schools, found that the children progressed better and preferred ordinary school as they felt it was less boring, less easy and offered a wider range of friendships. However, the child who needs a special school is the object of every effort to normalize, integrate, and to share and extend the quality and experience of life available to the able-bodied child. Many education authorities and organizations employ social workers attached to schools, both special and ordinary, to provide a co-ordinating service between school and family and between family and local agencies, voluntary and statutory. Many teachers arrange incoming and outgoing visits to compensate for possible lack of individual mobility and home stimulation, as well as provision of educational information and stimulation.

There is a need for co-operation with organizations and individuals who take over or continue care during the holiday periods, the hospitalization periods and at the end of the school life, and this includes the librarians in schools, hospitals and public libraries.

The help needed by those who are responsible for the care and teaching of handicapped children often depends upon where the child and worker are located geographically. In Britain, one source of help is at Pinderfields Hospital in Wakefield, where the Department of Neurology, Neuro-Surgery and Neurological Trauma has set up a National Demonstration Centre of aids for disabled people. The aim is to foster good rehabilitative services, and the disabled, and those who work with them, may telephone, write or visit for information and advice or to view the display of equipment and materials.

A toy library is offered also, based on an exhibition of equipment for handicapped children. Librarians and information therapists staff the Centre in addition to their work in the Postgraduate Medical Centre Library, all of which form part of the Wakefield Information Service for Medicine and Health Services. Similar centres can be found in London and a few other areas of the country and they also exist in America.

In some teachers' centres in Britain, and in their equivalent in America, Australia and some of the Scandinavian countries, teaching and learning aids are displayed. Reading machines, audio-visual equipment, and learning materials are there for use in remedial classes and in one-to-one sessions.

Children handicapped by hand or arm deficiency are handicapped in writing, and at secondary school where writing plays a more important part than in primary school, the child may fall behind in learning. The normal child writes at about fifteen to twenty words a minute. Severely physically handicapped children using POSSUM (Patient Operated Selector Mechanism) equipment can reach a speed only one or two words behind the child with normal writing. Thus, aids to the physical methods of learning and the physical use of books may be needed.

In schools for the physically handicapped there is an active use of books for learning purposes and there is often a liking for leisure reading, a quiet, physically passive recreation which, nevertheless, requires three conditions for functional and enjoyable success:

1 A reasonable reading proficiency.

2 A choice of books.
3 Access to them.

Many physically handicapped children spend a lot of time reading, and many who become handicapped after learning to read are fluent readers, with both deep and wide reading interests and developed taste. All those with whom I have spoken, indicate that though their bodies may be fettered their minds and imaginations are free, and they have the same interest in, and enjoyment of, books with themes of adventure and daring exploit, and books working out human relationships in fictional form, as able-bodied children.

Even the physical horizons of many handicapped children have become less limited, as schools and organizations are increasingly enabling children to travel much more extensively. Television, too, has widened their horizons and books and audio-visual materials complement the process. However, given that there are many physically handicapped children who are 'normal' readers and many able-bodied children who are less able readers, there are also disabled children who are retarded readers and these children need the materials and encouragement appropriate for educational retardation.

High interest, low vocabulary material is necessary for the slow learner, and a variety of media ensures that those who are able to learn in different ways by different means, can find the resources for pursuing those ways.

Paperbacks are inexpensive, lightweight and easily handled by children who may have difficulty in carrying heavy items and by children for whom size or bulk is a problem, in terms of being portable when moving about is difficult, or when wheelchairs have little carrying space. The physical properties of the average hardback book, including weight, size, page turning, typeface and angle of reading required, need to be considered in addition to the content, and in relation to the disabilities of the intended readership. In general, the library materials needed, including non-book material, are the same as those in the ordinary school or public library, but with a bias towards material for the less able. The organization of that material often differs.

In one special school I visited, the library was the responsibility of one of the teachers and at that time the stock was arranged in broad subject grouping, according to the project method of learning and teaching employed at the school. Where mobility is a problem, the advantage of this grouping is that children need only go to one section of the shelving to find the material required for the subject under study. The disadvantage lies in the fact that many information books are not limited to one subject and therefore the rest of the book's contents are not available for other subject work. Further disadvantages can be seen in terms of non-school work needs and interests, and in the training value for the independent use of other libraries. Where physically handicapped children may be limited to the school library because of distance from or difficulty in using a public library, there is perhaps a school responsibility to ensure the satisfaction of the wider non-school needs, and where one of the aims of education is to fit the child for adult life and for self help, it is important to see the school library in these terms also.

This comment is not a criticism of that particular school, because the work of an individual school should be geared to the known clientele and to specific financial and other constraints. But as a general comment, many special schools are small in terms of the number of students and the size of accommodation and there is a real danger that where a capitation allowance is the sole source of funds for library materials, the *quantity* of material purchaseable is generally limited, thus limiting the amount of choice available for the student. In such a situation the choice is further severely restricted by adopting the broad subject grouping approach.

Additionally, there is increasing recognition of the inter-relationship of many subjects, the fast growing quantity of multi-disciplinary information books and the urgent need to ensure as much independence as possible for the disabled child/adult. All these require the school to pay particular attention to its objectives regarding the library.

At one residential school I visited there was no centralized library, preference being given to classroom collections for the ninety children.

The reasons for this policy were given firstly, as enabling immediate access to the books during class time, for children who frequently needed to leave the classroom for all kinds of other purposes. Many needed to leave for an appointment with a doctor or therapist, for drugs, because of pain or illness, or simply for the reason of incontinence. Thus, by placing the majority of books in the classrooms a possible further disruption was avoided.

Secondly, because it is a residential school, the leisure time reading could be encouraged at other times by means of further recreational collections in the leisure areas and bedrooms.

It was at this school that I discovered that neither the teaching staff nor the regional librarian responsible for service to that school, were aware of the reading interests of the children. The regional librarian was able to visit the school once a year at the most, and the termly loan of books was carried out by regional headquarters staff selecting the material for children aged five to sixteen, unaware of their special needs and interests. The books were then delivered by van to the school. The teaching staff were concerned with their own subject materials and skills in the classroom, and the residential care staff for non-classroom time were not all knowledgeable about books for children and young people.

Many of the children read their own books brought from home or given by parents and friends, and the teenagers were reading adult paperbacks or pocketbooks. There were no adult books provided in either paperback or hardback on the bookshelves and the young people said they bought them when they were on vacation or they were gifts.

Since my visit, the regional librarian and the teaching staff have rectified these omissions, but there remains the at present insuperable difficulty for the librarian of maintaining a more frequent contact with each school, institution and service point in that region.

A third school exemplifying the varying ways in which schools organize library provision, is that of the Human Resources School at Albertson, Long Island, New York State. The school educates physically handicapped people, some of whom have other handicaps, and provides a wide range of materials – books, over 1,000 filmstrips, film loops, recordings, art slides, careers materials, periodicals, tapes and records, language kits, paperbacks and large print material, plus an information file on community and national resources and services available to the disabled.[3]

The scope of library provision depends on the kind of disability, the type of school, and the geographical location of the school in both education and public library service districts. These factors affect the need for a comprehensive stock or one which can be supplemented by a district school library service, or by public library and/or national library back-up, such as the Library of Congress Division for the Blind and Physically Handicapped in America and the National Listening Library in Britain.

Access to that provision is the third factor vital for successful reading, access physically to the library and, once in, to the materials in the library. I have visited two schools for physically handicapped children, both supposedly purpose built, which were split-level buildings, with steps rather than ramps, and with knob-handled doors rather than push-swing or electronically operated ones. Legislation in many countries now requires attention to accessibility for the disabled in public buildings, and this is covered in more detail in the section on design and planning of libraries, as is the arrangement within the library.

Access to the children's department of a public library is often difficult when this is situated upstairs or in the basement, without elevator access. But, once in, access to the activities of the children's library is easier, and special provision is not often needed. However, where there are to be crowds of children, as at a Book Fair, it is advisable to make special arrangements in order to (a) avoid jostling by the throng, (b) facilitate physical manœuvre by wheelchairs, (c) obtain the undivided attention of the exhibitors, and (d) enable the children to see the displays, which may not be at the height or location appropriate to their needs. For many years I helped to organize an annual Book Fair attended by thousands of children, and found out three years ago that a group of physically handicapped children, who were transported in a mini-bus from their school and conveyed by elevator to the exhibition hall, with half an hour to enjoy the displays of books, had to give up after a few minutes, as they were unable to move safely, or to see the books on show because of the crowds of children.

The next year, that school was sent an invitation to attend the opening ceremony and to browse in comfort before the first timetabled party of children arrived an hour later. The children's morale was raised and their interest increased, as a result of the honour of being at the ceremony and meeting the celebrity opener, and of having the opportunity of enjoying a vast range of books of all kinds.

There are many children whose physical handicap is such that they can cope with ordinary schooling, but around 24,000 children in Britain are officially diagnosed as being physically handicapped in such a way as to require special schooling, and each of these will benefit from books, whether they are intended for the purpose of education, for individual leisure pursuit, for group enjoyment or for one-to-one sharing.

Chapter Seven

The hospitalized child and the library

MOST CHILDREN in hospital are there for a short stay. In Britain around 1,300,000 children under fifteen were admitted to and discharged from hospital in 1972, 23 per cent were cases of tonsils and adenoids, and 16 per cent were accident, poisoning and violence cases. Some, in the total figure, were recurring admissions, but for all, the stay in hospital was likely to have social and psychological repercussions unless the stay was less than a week.[1]

Government health and education surveys indicate that in England and Wales over 8,000 children are in long-stay hospital care, most of them in psychiatric hospitals.

Libraries in mental institutions and hospitals are often inadequate and sometimes non-existent, even in countries with a strong library tradition such as Britain, Denmark and the USA, so the good examples already described in the chapter on the mentally handicapped child, rank as rare examples rather than as the norm.

What kind of hospital accommodation is available for children?

Paediatric care
Children's hospitals
Children's wards in a general or special hospital
Children's unit in a special department
In an adult ward
In a psychiatric hospital

Care for the mentally handicapped
Subnormality hospital
Subnormality ward in a general hospital.

Another categorization uses the terms

Maladjusted
Orthopaedic
General surgery and/or medical
General surgery, medical, orthopaedic, permanent handicaps, psychiatric disorder
Specialist hospitals, for example, epilepsy, plastic surgery, chest and heart.[2]

Special hospitals and special units can also include departments for children as in isolation hospitals, cancer and renal units. One of the most common potentially fatal diseases in children is cancer and in Britain 100 children in every million develop cancer each year. Though many are treated in regional clinics and day-bed units, many are admitted to cancer units for longer-term care.

Hospital schools
In British hospitals long-term stay involves not only the medical staff, but educational staff also, hospital schooling being a requirement for children who are able to undertake it. This is also the case for child patients in most other developed countries with free, compulsory state education.

The age range catered for in British hospital schools varies enormously, but the majority are in the range shown in Table 2.

TABLE 2

2 to 16 years	24·6%
2 „ 19 „	21·5%
5 „ 16 „	12·3%
5 „ 19 „	7·7%
3 „ 18 „	8·5%
3 „ 16 „	4·6%
4 „ 18 „	4·6%

The main anomaly here is in respect of the admission of children under 5 years of age, where there is no statutory obligation to educate. Approximately 45 per cent of the schools try to cater for these children but others have higher ages for admission to registers. It is possible, of course, that some hospitals may not admit children of 2, 3 or 4 years of age. At the other end of the age range it can be seen that many schools teach children over the age of 16 years. Five schools include adults (i.e. persons over 18 years of age) on their registers.[3]

Similar discrepancies between one school and another can be seen in Table 3, which shows the average number of children on roll in 102 schools and 18 units:

TABLE 3

Average Number on Roll

Head Teachers were asked to state the average number of children on roll in 1974. There were 120 replies to this question, made up of 102 Schools and 18 Units.

No. of pupils	*Schools*		*Units*		*Totals*
	ESN(S)	*Others*	*ESN(S)*	*Others*	
1– 20	1	15	–	10	26
21– 40	3	14	1	5	23
41– 60	12	19	1	1	33
61– 80	11	6			17
81–100	8	2			10
101–120	4	1			5
121–140	1	–			1
141–160	–	1			1
161–180	1	1			2
181–200	–	1			1
201 plus	1	–			1
	42	60	2	16	120

All schools/units except one had both boys and girls on roll.[4]

Such fluctuations in age range and number of children, cause immense problems for teachers in hospitals; problems of continuity, quantities of appropriate teaching material, use of limited teaching space, kinds and quantities of teachers for the varying numbers, ages, educational requirements and abilities of the child patients. To these problems can be added those caused by the medical requirements. Ward rounds, treatment periods, and visiting times (particularly in hospitals where there are no restrictions on visiting) normally take place during the day and therefore during school hours, so that the time available for actually getting down to learning is severely limited.

Other factors are the obvious ones of ill health, emotional disturbance at being away from home and family and, in the case of psychiatric and mentally handicapped children, the factor of degree of ability to undertake and profit from a teaching programme. Thus, the educational situation for children in hospital in any country is fraught with problems.

In those countries where education authorities have a statutory duty to provide education for all children and where there is a policy of funding school books and school libraries, the situation is not much better. A capitation allowance for these tends to be inadequate to cope with the difficulties of wide age range, fluctuating numbers and special requirements.

Few of the articles and books on hospital libraries published in any country pay attention to library provision for children in hospital. Eileen Cumming's 1971 article, 'Children in hospital: do they need a library service?'[5] recognized this, as did 'Sick and handicapped children: report of a joint meeting with the Youth Libraries Group in 1973';[6] similarly in the USA, where a useful six-page attempt is found in Eleanor Phinney's book *The Library and the Patient: an introduction to library services for patients in health care institutions*.[7]

Books in hospital

The teachers' union pamphlet, *Teaching in Hospital Schools*,[8] indicated some of the requirements for books and equipment.

> ... single copies of textbooks for children following specialized courses ... gramophone records for those whose need for oral practice of a foreign language cannot otherwise be met. A good supply of library books is particularly important because in hospital, children are likely to have more time than usual for reading; reading matter given by well-intentioned visitors may not always be suitable or adequate.

Experience suggests that the amount of time available for reading is no more in hospital than at home. Indeed, the constant noise and bustle, the presence of other children, medical staff, visitors and television, severely limit the amount of time for reading for many hospitalized children, whatever their disability, though there are always some who wish to, and are able to, 'lose' themselves in a book.

Where there is a centralized school library service, the hospital school can receive a regularly changed supply of books, both fiction and non-fiction, to supplement the school's own stock. Most of Britain's public library services operate a service to schools, including hospital schools. Other countries offer the same service to schools via the education service, which is usually separated from the public library service.

But the child in hospital is entitled to have the public library facilities he would have were he not hospitalized, and a 'patients' library as opposed to a 'school' library is available in most hospitals in the developed countries. How this is financed, organized and staffed varies widely from one hospital to another, in Britain and in other countries.

At a four-day course on 'Reading and the Handicapped Child', thirty school and children's librarians found that there were at least six different funding arrangements between them. Funding included:

1 Provision by the area health authority.
2 Special budget added to the children's book fund.
3 Education Department grants, half from the public library and half from the health authority.
4 General bookfund.
5 Regional Health Board.

The administration of a library service to children in hospital varied between:

1 Schools library service.
2 Children's library service.
3 Hospital and domiciliary department.
4 Hospital library.
5 Volunteers (including Red Cross, Women's Voluntary Service (WVS), and Friends of the Hospital).
6 None.

Such variation, of historical origin, is occasionally seen as the norm.

> Our pupils range in age from 2–18 years . . . the age range in each ward has widened with consequent repercussions from the point of view of teaching methods . . . It is evident that our pupils do not consider the library as a centrally placed room housing shelves of carefully catalogued books. They consider [it to be] the county

> library staff, who select and despatch boxes of books and also attend to individual requests through the postal service; the Red Cross librarian with her weekly book exchange from the mobile library trolley; the library shelves of the teachers in their ward annexe; and their source of supply in the teachers' staff room.[9]

While this is by no means the norm, either in attitude or practice, it does illustrate the lack of a national or even local policy towards the provision of books in hospitals, and while there are standards for hospital libraries, they require legislation to enforce them, and, in Britain, the USA, and most European countries, a complete reappraisal of the whole situation is needed, to rationalize and standardize where appropriate.

Where there is a hospital library and library staff there is often a division between the medical library and the patients' library in funding and administration. But whatever the demarcations, most hospitals have a section of the library for children's books, which may remain in the central area and/or be used to stock a trolley service or be deposited in or near to the children's wards or the teaching space.

The selection of books and other materials takes into account the wide age range, the educational needs, the recreational reading interests, the nature of the illness or disability, the method of distribution within the hospital, and the possibility of liaison with psychiatrists, therapists, social workers, careers/employment officers and parents. Gerald Bramley, in his book *Outreach: library services for the institutionalized, the elderly, and the physically handicapped*, says there are

> several ways in which books and other reading materials can help the younger patient who is confined to hospital for a lengthy period.
>
> 1 They can have a therapeutic effect. Reading as an activity ... can divert attention from illness or injury.
> 2 Some young people will be attending courses at college or university, and the librarian can in some cases act as an intermediary between patient and educational institute to obtain the books necessary to continue studies in hospital.
> 3 Occupational therapy; the librarian can arrange to supply books etc. related to this work.
> 4 Career material for alternative employment – with social workers and therapists.

5 Disabilities may prevent employment, so reading can be a recreational activity, an introduction to interests and activities, new hobbies or acquiring knowledge.[10]

For many children the experience of hospital is a shock and it is advocated that children should be prepared in advance for the experience, perhaps using the many picture books now available to 'smooth the path'.

For some children, reading familiar material helps to maintain a link with normality and for most, storytelling is a comforting, pleasant experience because it provides contact between the story reader or teller and the child, and transports the child to a known world or an acceptable fantasy world, thus taking his mind off a possibly frightening, hurtful or boring present world.

Storytelling in hospitals is frequently undertaken by a variety of people: by parents and family visitors, by teachers, by librarians, voluntary workers including, in some places in Britain, organized schemes for storytelling by members of the Federation of Children's Book Groups, by student teachers and student librarians, and occasionally by the medical and para-medical staff.

I recall taking a trolley service round the wards of a big teaching hospital in the north of England, many years ago, spending a lot of time in the plastic surgery ward where there were children who had been badly burned in fires or severely scalded or scarred in accidents, or who had congenital defects requiring plastic surgery.

One child burned and blinded by fire and requiring hospitalization and treatment for many years, was extremely responsive to the traditional stories, so many of which use 'visual' descriptive language.

Books in hospital can indeed be therapeutic, both for reading alone and reading aloud. The whole question of bibliotherapy is covered in an enormous quantity of literature on the theme. Rather than risk a shallow treatment of it here, I append a list of references for the interested reader to pursue in depth (Appendix 2). Bibliotherapy can be defined as a programme of planned and guided reading as treatment for emotional and other problems. Undertaken by psychologists and librarians trained in bibliotherapy, the aim is to give support, and to modify behaviour.

In addition to the books needed for study, and a selection of the general stock of children's books common to all children's libraries, many librarians serving children in hospital find that there is a need for and an interest in 'easy' reading books for both young and teenage patients. For example, large print books, annuals, magazines, reference books, pop-up and tactile books, picture books and paperbacks and books suitable for reading aloud by parents and other storytellers. Cassettes of music, story or instruction are also popular, the use of headphones being a requirement on the ward, though in dayrooms there may be communal enjoyment of recorded material.

Mention has already been made, in the chapter on mentally handicapped children, of the interest in music exhibited by many in hospitals for the mentally handicapped, and I have seen this in special schools and in the children's own homes also. In a general hospital in Copenhagen there is extensive provision of music in one form or another for the patients, in the belief that the audio-visual format is an integral part of a library service, and supported by the researched evidence that music can be therapeutic.

The provision of taped stories and talking books, and the use of films and slides are also evident in some hospitals.

In some countries the hospital library is also the public library, either officially or unofficially. In the Herlev hospital in Copenhagen the library is organized as a branch of the local public library and is open from 10.00 am to 3.30 pm every day; it operates a ward service also, and a medical library, all from a stock of 10,000 books, 1,000 cassettes, 1,000 records, 100 magazines and 500 talking books. Although there is no children's ward, there is a nursery for the children of hospital staff and they use the children's section of the library.

Similarly in Sheffield, England, two large hospitals, a psychiatric and a general hospital, share a site and are served by a small branch library which is owned and staffed by the Sheffield Area Health Authority. Two staff provide a ward service to all parts of the hospital every morning and staff the branch library in the afternoons. Used by medical, administrative, nursing and manual staff, and by the psychiatric patients, the public library service regularly provides and exchanges the general stock of about 6,000 volumes and buys books and audio-visual material for the medical collection, on mainly psychiatric subjects. The Consultants' Library is provided from Sheffield Area Health Authority funds and the public library has no responsibility for it.

From this kind of organized public/hospital service, to an informal joint arrangement operating in a country hospital in the Philippines, is a big step. The Philippines hospital has only a few medical books, a hundred or so ordinary books and a handful of children's books, for its few staff and many patients. With a Peace Corps worker and the backing of the administrator, efforts are being made to increase the library stock, not only for the hospital population, but for the use of the local population also, in the absence of any kind of public library service. As is the custom, the patients' family stay with him while he is in hospital, and they, and visitors, could make good use of a collection of books in the hospital. No educational facilities are available for the children in hospital so that books become an important vehicle for either beginning or continuing education.

It makes sense for the hospital patients' library to function in this dual role and it is a potential answer in many cases where there is a lack of one or the other, given a satisfactory arrangement for funding and staffing.

Whether the librarian is on the permanent staff of the hospital, comes into the hospital from an external organization, or is peripatetic, there is a common professional interest and need, which is fostered and helped by membership of a national professional body.

In several countries the national library association has a special section concerned with hospital libraries, providing a forum for meetings, exchange of information and promotion of service; for example, the Medical Health and Welfare Libraries Group of the Library Association in Britain and the Association of Hospital and Institutional Libraries in the USA; the International Federation of Library Associations (IFLA) also has a section called Library Services to Hospital Patients and Handicapped Readers.

Much of the work of a librarian in a hospital is determined by the nature of the hospital's administration and funding; the nature of the medical and health conditions it serves; the amount of liaison possible between all who have a responsibility for the welfare and recovery of the child; and the status accorded to the librarian's post in the official establishment and in the eyes of the co-workers. Much of the work is aided by observing protocol within the hospital, and by maintaining friendly co-operation with the ward sisters and the teachers, and much of the work is effected by demonstrating that books can be therapeutic in many ways.

Chapter Eight

The handicapped child and the public library

THE HANDICAPPED CHILD may have arrived at the public library in the same way as the ordinary child. He travels by himself, is brought by a member of his family, is accompanied by a teacher or helper, or is in a group or class of children visiting once or regularly.

The ease with which he does any of these things depends upon the severity of his disability, the distance from the library, the availability of public or private transportation and the willingness of someone to accompany him, and though some of these also apply to the ordinary child, the distinction lies in the extra time and effort involved where the handicapped child is concerned.

Given these mainly physical difficulties, a further problem arises over attitudinal obstacles. Many parents of handicapped children mention *their* own fear of taking their children to a public place where (a) the child's behaviour may not accord with that required in a particular place, (b) the public may be rude, hostile, or embarrassed by the presence of an obviously handicapped child, or, and possibly worse, react adversely to the behaviour of a child who is *not* obviously visibly handicapped, and (c) the officials or staff at the place visited may be hostile or unhelpful.

Such attitudes on the part of parent or library staff may prevent the child from access to the public library far more effectively than distance, transport, or the barriers inherent in the design and layout of the library, which are discussed in the chapter on design.

Public attitudes can be helped over a long period by public

education, since hostility and embarrassment are usually born of a fear engendered by ignorance or lack of understanding. Parents can be helped too, by ensuring that library staff are not also ignorant and lacking in understanding of the nature of the problems and needs of the various disabilities, and can act and react helpfully and sympathetically.

As far as the library staff are concerned, this should spring from a recognition of these needs in the library system's policies. In library planning and management policies, the handicapped should have a place in the total scheme, to the extent of specifying this in written documents.

Throughout the world much legislation has been passed which omits to specify either children or the handicapped, on the grounds that the legislation automatically refers to *all* people. But a look at the legislation and then at the actual practice shows that internationally, in most cases, it is necessary to specify the category in order to ensure extra, or even equal provision. Some countries have set up national committees to look into library provision, for example:

(a) NORWAY. In 1973 the Norwegian government established a select committee to study questions relating to the supply of literature and the provision of public library services for the handicapped.[1] It proposed an annual production of thirty books in large type; picture books with sign language text for deaf children; and braille-style books for blind children. It suggested that an advisory council should be appointed, to:

1 Select the books to be published in braille and on tape.
2 Select the books to be produced as video programmes.
3 Promote talking newspapers and magazines, and braille versions of these.
4 Promote reading aids.
5 Take full responsibility for library activities for the blind and deaf in Norway.

(b) NIGERIA. The Nigerian National Advisory Council for the Blind was set up in 1960, with a library of braille books and a braille press. It sent:

1 A questionnaire to state and public libraries in Nigeria.

2 A questionnaire to schools and institutions for the handicapped.

Three of 19 state libraries provide facilities; only one school had audio-visual materials and most had only small classroom collections of books. Constraints were funding and a lack of trained librarians.

> Answers to the following questions and many others will have to be provided. How can one determine the needs of the handicapped library-wise? Will these be related to their vocations, everyday living, education needs? What factors inhibit their use of library facilities? How feasible is it for them to use conventional library resources or would special services have to be provided?[2]

In England, the 1970 Chronically Sick and Disabled Persons Act requires public libraries to provide a service to the handicapped, and in England, as in some other countries, the directors of library services will say that handicapped people *are* served. Most would agree that they do not and perhaps cannot ensure that the handicapped person has an *equal* opportunity to benefit from the normal services, and even regionalized schools library services often omit or give a lesser service to special schools.

Often the distribution of full-time professional school librarians is conditioned largely by the number of pupils, thus depriving special schools of a skilled librarian, since most have a much smaller pupil population.

Lack of specific reference within the legislation means that the handicapped child is faced with another handicap, that of being denied qualified help in selecting reading materials. However, with or without legislation, some public libraries make an internal policy statement, as in the oft-quoted example of Philadelphia's public library:

> Our first job is to create a favorable climate of opinion towards the handicapped; our second is to entertain and inform many crippled and blind people, both children and adults; and our third is to guide those specialized people who work with the handicapped through our resources of books, periodicals, documents and films.[3]

Standards are often only little better unless backed by

legislation and by funds. The American Library Association's *Standards for Library Services for the Blind and Visually Handicapped* (1967) suggest that the community library must have 'qualified staff making communication with the visually handicapped,' admitting that though there is a cost factor in a community with a small population, there is a requirement to provide resource files, information registers and special activities.

The Standards advocate the employment of a full-time librarian for each hundred children after the first 100 in special schools for the visually handicapped. If this standard were to be applied to a public library authority service to the handicapped, the employment of a specialist librarian would be needed in many of the larger urban authorities where the incidence of handicap is greater than in rural areas, and in areas where, for various reasons, there are a number of special schools.

In some British library authorities where the librarian in charge of school library services has the title and status of adviser, it may be easier to liaise with the special education adviser on library matters concerning handicapped children. But in any country, communication and co-operation between public librarians, those who organize school libraries, and those who teach special children, is vital if the child is to benefit from the public library during childhood, and, more importantly, during adulthood, when many of the props of school and health authorities are taken away.

As indicated in the section on further education, in many areas there is a lack of a 'whole-life' care plan for the handicapped, particularly the mentally handicapped, educationally, institutionally *and* in library services. Young people, transferring at the age of eighteen or twenty from a residential school to an adult home, hostel or hospital, are likely to get a much reduced library service; this is equally true for the young handicapped person who leaves school for an adult life, living at home, working in sheltered workshops, or in a job in the community.

The staffing involved in serving the known needs, requires a policy of appointment, deployment and staff training related to the local situation.

Some library systems operate a special services division with specialist staff, for example in the USA, Cincinnati and Hamilton County Public Library has an Exceptional Children's Department, and the District of Columbia Public Library has a Co-ordinator of Services for the Hearing Impaired. In Britain, services for handicapped adults tend to be the responsibility of the public library's service to the housebound, as in Sheffield Metropolitan District, or of the Domiciliary Service as in Cornwall County and Rothwell Metropolitan District, or of the Hospital and Special Services Librarian as at Doncaster; whereas public library service to handicapped children is usually left to the individual librarian's own initiative, as far as the child out of school is concerned, and to the public library's, or education authority's, service to schools, including special schools.

The Special Services divisions in the USA, often have an outreach programme, as at Virginia Beach, Virginia, where the special librarian contacts parents, educators and eligible children; speaks to civic and service organizations; sets up displays in libraries and schools; takes part in television talks and news shows on the service; and is listed with the City Speaker's Bureau. The National Library Service for the Blind and Physically Handicapped, in the Library of Congress in the USA, co-ordinates a network of regional and sub-regional services based on public libraries and other libraries at which special materials and equipment can be obtained. Whatever the local administrative process and method employed, it should be the result of a policy decision based on known need and potential use. How is the need gauged?

Information can be obtained from the education sources on the number of children in special education in the community, the types of disability and the distribution amongst kinds of school or institution. Similarly, the hospital authorities have statistical information on the children in their care. Professional and voluntary organizations concerned with the welfare of handicapped children, may also be approached for information on what they see as the library needs of the children, whether they are special education teachers' organizations, parents' groups, or national organizations concerned with specific handicaps. The library can ascertain what percentage of the children can actually visit a library, determine for what purpose and in what way they would use the library, and assess how many are unable to visit and for what reason. A look at what resources the library already possesses, suitable for any known special needs, leads on to a consideration of from whence the librarian could supplement those resources.

When many library systems have difficulty in satisfying the needs and wants of normal children who form the majority of library users, any service that requires special or extra staff, stock or time, may be considered a minority service and left until conditions are deemed viable. If in existence, they may be neglected or starved of resources, to favour the majority, unless legislation, standards, and internal policy statements require such a special service to be maintained.

In Yorkshire, in the north of England, the Youth Libraries Group (Yorkshire Branch) of the British Library Association carried out a survey, *Public Library Facilities for Handicapped Children in Yorkshire: survey and directory*,[4] with the following aims:

1 To find out what facilities libraries in Yorkshire provide for handicapped children, as regards materials, activities, services, staffing, design of buildings and special equipment.
2 To find out what societies concerned with helping these children think public libraries could provide.
3 To help libraries and societies to be aware of each other and to promote liaison between them.

A questionnaire (Appendix 4) was sent to the eleven library authorities in Yorkshire, with 100 per cent return. A different questionnaire (Appendix 5) was sent to the local representatives of twenty-five national societies concerned with handicapped children, and sixteen returned the completed questionnaire.

The answers from the societies, plus interesting accompanying letters in some cases, made useful suggestions.

Material supplied by the libraries included large print books for retarded or language impaired readers, talking books, cassettes and records. The societies suggested a need for discs, pictures (to help speech and language development), toy libraries, work cards, games and play materials, project materials for children having home tuition, braille books and arithmetic type boards.

The selection of appropriate materials for handicapped readers is covered in outline in my chapter on children's libraries in the *Manual of Library Economy*[5] and in detail in the next chapter here. But emphasis can be laid on the use of non-fiction by many handicapped children. As most have some difficulty with reading and may not be able to cope fluently, and therefore enjoyably, with fiction, many, particularly boys, find both pleasure and information in non-fiction. Classes of handicapped children visiting the public library to borrow books, mostly choose information books.

The need for an information service was stressed by three societies, Dr Barnardo's, the Association for Therapeutic Education and the Toy Libraries Association, who suggested that information and literature on voluntary aid societies, welfare benefits, and local professional help, should be made available to parents of the handicapped, to teachers, and to leaders of playgroups. This can include journals and newsletters of societies for the handicapped; catalogues of national library services for the handicapped; information files and leaflets with names and addresses of local and national societies concerned with particular handicaps; trade catalogues of audio-visual equipment and reading aids, such as page turners and magnifying aids, and information on radio and TV programmes for and about handicapped children. In the USA, Brooklyn Public Library provides a packet of information materials for parents of handicapped children needing special services.

An important information service is that of providing reading lists and select bibliographies of print and non-print materials, to cater for the needs of particular groups or individuals. Such lists serve to identify one or more of the following specific subjects: treatment of subjects, levels of readability, types of physical format, fictional themes related to handicaps, and information books and articles *about* handicaps. Some of these are exemplified later in the bibliographies and appendices. In general, the aim is to inform the child, or adult helper, of what is appropriate out of a mass of material; to help him to locate it quickly in the catalogue or on the shelf, or to use it as a selection guide for setting up, or adding to, the special stock of a school or other library.

The form in which the information is given, can vary from a 'dial-the-library' service to a local radio or television programme, all of which are utilized by many public libraries in several countries. Many also have talking newspapers, though in some cases the actual work is done by voluntary bodies. There are twenty-five in Sweden and about twelve in Britain, and though they are not aimed at children, they offer much that is interesting and useful to the older handicapped child and teenager. The equipment and space needed for these is discussed in the chapter on design and equipment.

Liaison was stressed in the Yorkshire survey, which found that most of the public library systems liaised regularly and predominantly with:

1 Special schools.
2 Social services departments.
3 Education departments.
4 Health services.
5 Societies/organizations.

There was agreement on the need for particular services, for example, home delivery of materials, and deposit collections. Seven of the eleven public libraries maintain deposit collections in a total of eighty-five special schools, eleven day centres and hostels, five hospitals, three playgroups and nurseries, and a toy library.

Library activities were surveyed and six of the eleven libraries offered story sessions, both integrated with normal children and special programmes in hospitals and residential schools; class visits to the library, and exhibitions of children's work in the library.

The societies supported the provision of these and suggested that there was also a need for 'creative and developmental activities to help discriminatory and manipulative skills'. There was a stated need for holiday activities, particularly for children from special schools, who tend to lapse or regress during holiday breaks from school routine. The following is an example of a holiday activity.

During the school holidays a children's librarian at Bishop's Stortford visited a playgroup for mentally handicapped children to tell stories, do fingerplays and join in other activities. She writes:

> The children vary in age from about four to eleven, and have wide ranging mental ages too, so presentation and content have to be equally varied and carefully considered. An interesting aspect is that the children of the playgroup leaders attend, which is a benefit both to them and to the handicapped children.
>
> It's exhausting, but great fun, and you have to keep your wits about you – my glasses were grabbed in the first five minutes. It's not the sort of place you wear your best clothes, either – I've come back covered in flour, treacle finger prints and green paint. The playgroup leaders are delighted to have any help they can get, and it's good for the children to meet somebody different. The noisier your repertoire the better, and fingerplays have to be done a bit more slowly, with help, to get the correct fingers. Another good point about it is that it spreads the word you're willing to help, to other playgroups.[6]

The usual activities carried out in many public library children's departments to exploit and promote the stock, are useful for either normal or disabled children and should be undertaken with both without discrimination, or they can be adapted to suit the requirements of a special group.

Space, staff available, time, and occasionally money, determine the extent of activity possible in a given library, but the following can be organized in a school, institutional or public library for the benefit of the children, and I have personally organized all of these in various libraries in a number of countries, and have seen them operating in other libraries and countries.

- Art and handicraft groups
- Book review schemes
- Book weeks
- Bookworm clubs
- Brains trusts
- Chess clubs
- Class visits
- Concerts by children and others
- Creative writing sessions
- Drama and poetry groups
- Ethnic national days
- Family reading groups
- Film shows
- Magazine or newsheet
- Quizzes
- Radio and television sessions
- Scrapbooks
- Storyhours
- Talks by authors/illustrators
- Talks by local speakers

To these can be added possible invitations to the several clubs operating in Britain (there are equivalents in other countries), in which the able and the disabled socialize; for example, PHAB, the Association of Clubs for the Physically Handicapped and Able Bodied; Gateway, the Association of Clubs for the Mentally Handicapped and Mentally Able; and Breakthrough Trust, the Association of Clubs for the Hearing and the Hearing Impaired.

The planning required for the visits of handicapped children to the library in groups, involves consideration of a number of factors:

1 *Physical* The location of the activity: separate room, corner of the branch library, access for wheelchairs, toilet facilities. These may affect whether the children *can* visit, type of activity and the number possible.
2 *Transport* The means by which the children arrive at the library may affect how tired/wet/warm/cold they are on arrival and how long they can stay, if dependent on public transport.
3 *Children* Different handicaps have attendant problems, for example, the need for tissues for mopping up; interruption of the programme for toilet or behaviour; setting up of seating and equipment appropriate to the handicap.
4 *Materials/activities* Advance preparation is needed for story-telling/reading, watching films/slides, painting and glue-ing activities, shadow play, drama, games, information searching and book choosing.
5 *Staff* The ratio of staff to children is a factor which affects the supervision, amount of help that can be given, and the type or activity. As the children probably pass through the library building, all staff should be briefed.

The special aspects of reading and telling stories are identified in the chapter on storytelling, but emphasis is laid here on the universal appeal of stories read or told to all children.

Where library premises do not permit class visits or the children are not able to make the journey, the librarian may visit the school or institution with a similar programme; there are many examples of this, directly mentioned in previous chapters, but a few of many general examples of practice can be given here. In England, a librarian in Luton, Bedfordshire, regularly visits special schools to give book talks and to display a range of books for the children to browse through, and a librarian in Hertfordshire has a weekly story and book time at a school for mentally handicapped children.

In Tasmania, a librarian has become a professional storyteller to handicapped children and in Jamaica, a school for physically handicapped children receives regular visits from library staff. These examples can be duplicated many times over.

In addition to the work done by the children's librarian, there is the major work of the schools library service, which in England and Wales is normally administered by the public library. The actual services are the same as those offered in Scotland, the USA, and Australia by the school library services, administered by the education authorities. Whatever the origin of the administration, the services to special schools follow the same pattern as those to ordinary schools, for example:

1 Loan of materials to supplement the school's own stock, either long-term or short-term.
2 Advisory and information service to teachers and school librarians on the organization of the library, materials and services, bibliographical aid, educational information service and, in some cases, peripatetic staffing.
3 Maintenance of a centralized pool of material and equipment for loan, display, reference.
4 Co-ordination of teacher-librarians/professional librarians working in the schools within the system.
5 In-service training.

While these services are likely to be available to all schools, the specialist nature of much of the stock, advice and work required by special schools, demands special attention and in some countries is therefore separated into a special services division. In the USA, the Bureau of Education for the Handicapped operates Regional Resource Centers and Direction Service Centers, mostly situated in universities, and these centres supply materials and information to the area. In Britain, most teachers' centres within a region contain information and materials in varying quantities.

Standards for school library resource centres, often also contain standards for centralized co-ordinative library services, though the special aspects of these receive little detailed coverage.

The average librarian working with children in a public library, will not have received much, if any, educational training in the library needs of special children, and many will not have experienced these in practice either.

Some programmes of professional librarianship education contain an elective course on library service to the handicapped, some have integrated the subject into the general course, and some include the special aspects of library service to the handicapped child in the children's librarianship/literature option. Others incorporate the subject into medical/hospital librarianship courses or into special education electives, while some require a dual qualification in teaching and librarianship before allowing contact with the special child.

Because the nature of most professional librarianship first courses precludes much specialization in depth, some countries' library education institutions offer master's or doctoral programmes, enabling research or other specialization to be undertaken, and a glance at the doctoral programmes and lists of theses of many American universities indicates the range of specialization in the subject area of the special child.

So the average librarian in the public library is unlikely to have in-depth knowledge or experience, and thus requires in-service or extra-mural training, but the growing awareness in many countries that there *are* special needs has led to programmes of on-going training.

Many library authorities in Britain have such a programme for their staff, and the needs of handicapped readers find a place in the programme from time to time. Similarly, in other countries such attempts to add to knowledge are to be found. Recent examples include those of Margaret Dunkle of the State Library of Victoria, who organized state-wide courses on services and materials required by physically handicapped, deaf and blind children, for librarians working with the children; and Ann Parker of Hertfordshire County Library Services to Children and Schools, who organized a similar course on 'the library and the handicapped child' for children's librarians, teacher-librarians and education personnel in the county. Many individual American library systems inform and update their staff in this way and, as discussed in the first chapter, there are increasing numbers of co-operative courses/conferences put on by national or local bodies.

The need for co-operation between the various categories of people who work with the children is vital, and an example of such co-operation can be seen in County Durham, England, where the Nurse Training Unit at the large Aycliffe Hospital for the mentally handicapped, liaises with the local library service in a mutual training effort, whereby lectures are given to student librarians by the Senior Nurse Tutor, and visits to hospital libraries for instruction on libraries, are arranged for all student nurses. The latter also make books as part of their projects and there is the opportunity to tape story reading and patients' comments and stories specifically in the local dialect.

In-service training is part of the policy of service to the handicapped within a library system. No amount of statement on the principle of provision within the library's objectives document, will cover the inadequacy of a service attempted by staff who have not been introduced to the problems and needs, and who have not been informed and trained in the ways of alleviating library problems and satisfying library needs.

In general terms, the stock, service and access suggested by the societies is already provided by some 'good' library systems, but taking public library services as a whole – though intentions are often good and recognition of the need is often evident – good practice is patchy both throughout a particular library system and nationally, in the majority of countries.

The good librarian recognizes that within the normal stock there are types of material that can be exploited for the handicapped, and that the literary and format boundaries employed in traditional children's librarianship must be extended to cater for types and levels of material needed by the handicapped child.

The public library needs to facilitate access by the handicapped child to the appropriate items in the following list:

1 All children's and young adult stock.
2 Books for backward readers, large print books, cassettes and music.

3 Sensory books, such as scratch and sniff, pop-up, touch books, mirror and overlay books.
4 Durable format, such as cloth books, board books, laminated cards and pictures.
5 Games and toys.

Access is needed for those who work with handicapped children, to:

1 Journals and newsletters of organizations concerned with the handicapped.
2 Information material on national and local library services for the handicapped.
3 Information material on national and local societies concerned with particular handicaps.
4 Trade catalogues of equipment, aids, etc.
5 Information/lists/catalogues of general books, and books specifically about handicaps.

To obtain and promote the above, means liaising with the organizations concerned, with the children, and with the teachers and parents, and this is all part of the librarian's job, which is to participate in the socialization process and the educational and recreational development of the handicapped child, and to guide him towards independence in adult life.

Chapter Nine

Toy libraries

THE HANDICAPPED CHILD, deprived of the physical or mental ability to use the conventional book, is often in great need of other stimuli and some librarians understand that knowledge is not confined to the printed or aural word.

Toys and games are available in many public library children's departments and I have seen these in West Germany, Czechoslovakia, Australia, America and England. The toy library is very much in evidence in some countries and is administered in varying ways, some involving public libraries directly, in provision of space or staff in the library, as in Brighton, England, where the first toy library was established, the brain child of John Allen, and Newcastle, Australia; others are run by voluntary bodies in co-operation with the children's librarian; some are organized by parents, playgroup leaders, speech therapists, health visitors, social workers, or psychologists, as at Nottingham University.

Some are housed in mobile libraries, branch libraries, clinics, day centres for mothers and babies, special schools, hospitals, nursery schools, church halls or community centres, and their funding varies from reliance on individual donations, through institutional funds to finance from local authority funds.

The staffing of the toy library varies from volunteer parents and helpers to psychologists and therapists, and is to some extent determined by the host body within which the toy library operates, and any stipulations laid down as to who may borrow the toys. Some toy libraries are for children with a specific handicap, often mental handicaps, some for a wide range of physically and mentally handicapped and some include the socially handicapped child also.

The role of the professional librarian who assists with such a library, is to meet the helpers, to share concern for the handicapped child; to indicate suitable book stock to be incorporated into the toy library stock; to provide lists of such for parents who borrow the toys; to advise on sources of information about services and organizations for the handicapped; to provide aid with transport; to offer expertise on such matters as loan procedures, cataloguing of items and display of toys; to ensure that in-service staff training contains an introduction to the toy needs of parents and children, and to publicize the existence of the toy library.

The majority of toy libraries are linked one way or another to the Toy Libraries Association in England, at Seabrook House, Wyllyotts Manor, Darkes Lane, Potters Bar, Herts, EN6 2HL, which publishes a journal *Ark*, several guides such as *The ABC of Toys*, *Toys for Children with Hearing, Speech and Language Difficulties*, *Encouraging Language Development*, *How to start a Toy Library*, etc. The Association's publications and advice have been sent to many countries where individuals and groups wanted to set up toy libraries.

Some examples of existing toy libraries will indicate the range of administration and provision to be found in many countries; for instance, Newcastle Public Library and Newcastle and Hunter Valley Toy Libraries Association in Australia operate in the following way:

The public library provides accommodation, books and organizational facilities like accessioning and cataloguing.

The Toy Libraries Association selects the stock of toys and staff, and provides voluntary staff, mainly with social work, therapy and teaching skills.

Classification is by an adaptation of the Bristol Toy Libraries Association's system, using:

A	for Activity
B	for Baby play
CM	for Communication
CR	for Co-ordination
D	for Discrimination
E	for Expression
F	for Fun and games
G	for General multi-function toys

Cataloguing is in the following style:

1 Name of toy (given by maker or catalogue).
2 Name of maker.
3 Collation.
4 Contents note.
5 Accession detail, call number and tracing notes.[1]

The service is aimed at mentally and physically handicapped children.

In Britain, the Nottingham University Toy Library began as a research project in the Psychology Department, funded by the National Fund for Research into Crippling Diseases, but developed into a full toy library staffed by psychologists, funded by Nottinghamshire County Council, and serving a wide range of handicap, mainly children of pre-school age.

There is an appointments system whereby the children and parents attend at a given time, during which the child is observed at play, the parents discuss him with the psychologists (all of whom have experience in teaching or therapy), and toys appropriate to the developmental level are chosen, to be returned at the next appointment about a month later. After-school sessions for older children are held monthly and parents' open evenings occasionally. Pamphlets and books are available for parents and other interested adults and three audio-tapes, (a) Nottingham University's *Toy Libraries for Handicapped Children*, (b) *Choosing Toys and Play Activities for the Young Handicapped Child*, and (c) *Playthings for the Handicapped Child*, are obtainable from the Medical Recording Service Foundation, Kitts Croft, Writtle, Chelmsford, Essex.

Also in Britain, the Institute for the Deaf, in Leeds, has a toy library, the brain child of a member of the local Parents Association for Cerebral Palsy Education. Open twice a month, the library offers, free, toys chosen to improve mobility and co-ordination.

A toy library in a hospital is exemplified by that at the National Demonstration Centre in Pinderfields Hospital, Wakefield, England, where professional advice on the best toys for individual children is given by clinical psychologists. The Social Services Department of the local authority funded the initial purchase of toys, and local schools and businesses have agreed to make and donate more.

In Holland, the city of Alphen ann den Rijn Toy Library is funded partly by the city and partly by donations, and is staffed by many volunteers. Apart from providing toys for nearly one hundred families and two children's hospitals, the staff organize school evenings for local special schools, and exhibitions. Groups of volunteers make toys from wood and sewing materials and there is a reading club which makes the story tapes for children aged one to eight who are ill or handicapped. A survey in Australia[2] revealed many varieties in that State alone, and in other countries also hundreds of small libraries are organized by small groups of parents, with donations of money and toys, which provide a much needed service in their locality.

What kinds of toy are appropriate for the handicapped child? The following is a list of such toys, which also indicates the purposes they can serve:

1 Mobiles: because these move they are useful for both developing the children's eye movements and for holding their attention.
2 Carousels, seesaws, squeaky toys: these are an endless source of fascination for children, and, once again, can be used for capturing the children's attention.
3 Rattles, balls, blocks, stacking rings and rag books: these are all toys which can be handled and fingered and which can therefore aid the development of co-ordination and a sense of touch.
4 Trundle toys, bobcart, special scooters, etc: these toys can be used to aid mobility.
5 Threading toys and hammer toys: these toys can be used to develop hand/eye co-ordination.
6 Bricks and Lego: these are constructional toys and thus present the children with a challenge, encouraging them to think and stimulating mental exercise.
7 Sorting boxes, dimensional puzzles, dominoes, lotto, jigsaws: again, these toys present the children with a challenge and encourage the development of various kinds of discrimination (matching, sorting, grading by size, colour, shape, etc).

8 Word games, telephones, conversation pictures, talking pictures, bubble blowing, etc: these can all be used to develop speech and language.
9 Noughts and crosses, number puzzles: these can be used to develop numeracy.
10 Tambourines, balls, musical boxes: these provide the children with enjoyment and can be therapeutic.

The way in which the loan of toys is administered varies, and full details are given in the Toy Libraries Association pamphlet, *How to Set Up a Toy Library*, but basically the aspects to be covered, as with books, include the source of supply; accessioning; borrowers' files; record of loans; display of stock, whether wall hanging, table, shelf or floor display; care of toys, e.g. hygiene via clear polyurethane non-toxic varnish, self-adhesive film, washing, etc; carriers for portable items, whether net bags, perspex bags, cartons or wooden boxes; repair of toys, using local volunteers in schools and the community; and publicity.

Sources of supply commercially are numerous in Britain and there are catalogues from such bodies as the Design Council, *Design Centre Guide to Play Equipment for Young Children*; Early Learning Centre, Oxford; *Toys and Ideas for Children When Ill*, James Galt and Company Limited, London; Health Education Council's *Toys and Playthings: what kind . . . at what age?*; and Nottingham University Toy Library has a list of nearly fifty designers, manufacturers and suppliers of toys and a select list of recommended toys (with names of suppliers).

The concept of a toy library complements the concept of a print or audio-visual library, that of availability of materials which will stimulate the imagination, aid language development, inform, and provide pleasure. As such the toy library has a valid place in the spectrum of library provision.

Chapter Ten

Storytelling and the handicapped child

STORYTELLING to any child, at any time, is never less than profitable in a multiplicity of ways, but for the handicapped child there are extra or compensatory benefits, which should provide the librarian, teacher or other storyteller with every justification for undertaking it. A formal justification is often needed, psychologically, by those who tell stories because it is such a pleasant activity for both the teller and the listener that many teachers and librarians feel guilty at spending a lot of time on it (teachers particularly), and many in authority who observe the time spent on this, consider the whole event a 'twee', trivial source of entertainment and the people who do it, 'soft'.

But storytelling is, in fact, a multiple educational experience which carries within it enjoyment, a boon for educationalists, in that enjoyment is a great motivator for beginning, pursuing and continuing anything.

The most obvious benefit is the *language stimulus*. Learning to read depends to a large extent on the child's experience of language, heard and seen. Many handicapped children have a limited experience of language because they may not have been exposed to the 'normal' child's experience of language in the home, in the street, amongst the peer group, and on radio and television.

Depending upon the disability, it is likely that the child will have been spoken to in a simplified way, thus limiting his knowledge of spoken language, and, if mentally impaired or deaf, the words normally unconsciously heard as indirect speech will be lacking. The words children normally see in books, comics, magazines, advertisements, and in shops and on transport may be lacking in the vocabulary of the child with a visual, perceptual or conceptual impairment, so that the young child's normal experience of language is likely to be limited in the handicapped child.

Storytelling can increase the child's vocabulary by presenting known words and new words understandably in the story context. The sentence patterns used in storytelling are likely to be different from, or an extension of, the kind of spoken language the child *has* heard, thus extending his experience and knowledge of such language, which will help him when he sees it in the printed form in a book.

The *audio-stimulus* comes to children who may have *heard* sounds and words but not have actively *listened* to them. The difference between the normal conversational inflections of the voice and the tones used in storytelling may also convey meaning.

The audio stimulus may come from group listening as distinct from one-to-one storytelling. Both the teller and the listener may adopt a different, if unconscious, approach to group storytelling and the young child who may not have had to listen in company with others will perhaps reap more information and comprehension from the responses of others in the group (though there are, of course, dangers of distraction by the behaviour of others).

Visual stimulus comes from the use of picture books, films, puppets, objects and other visual media, and indeed from the teller himself, via his facial expression and actions. These are all stimuli to perception, discrimination and information.

The importance of visual stimulus cannot be overstressed, both as a means of attracting and maintaining attention and of conveying information, which gives meaning to the words and knowledge and experience.

Experience is a key factor in justifying both reading and storytelling. The child's own experience can be reinforced by the well chosen story, whether it is a physical, geographical or emotional experience, and his limited experience can be widened as he is presented with new experiences in story form. Such vicarious experience can be exciting or calming, compensatory or complementary, and informative, whether relating to the real world or the world of imagination.

The *therapeutic effect* is well known to all storytellers and to those who carefully practise bibliotherapy.

The good story evokes a response; recognition, identification, fear, love, tension, relief. The good story educates the emotions by enabling them to be practiced vicariously, and therefore, with most children, safely. It educates the imagination and, both emotionally and imaginatively, can enable the older child particularly, to feel that he is not alone in his problems, someone else has been there before him.

Socialization is also possible in the storytelling process. Stories introduce the child to words, mores, morals and models of life and behaviour, potential civilizing experiences. The environment of storytelling is socializing in that it requires a relationship between the teller and the listener, an interaction. Whoever the good storyteller is, librarian, teacher, parent or other, a bond is created, whether one-to-one or in a group.

The group storytelling, whether in class or in the library, is a communal experience, education in assimilable form in pleasant circumstances, in the group's safety and providing both communal and individual pleasure.

The provision of such enormous benefit, of course, requires preparation and thought for achievement with some handicapped children.

Some of the handicaps require attention to particular aspects and practices.

Storytelling and the mentally handicapped child

I watched a teacher reading a story to her class of eight mentally handicapped seven- and eight-year-olds, all sitting at a round table, with the teacher holding the book, pages facing outwards, against her chest. The children continually leaned across the table to touch the teacher, the book, and particular pictures, or part of a picture. The teacher pointed to the relevant aspects of the picture as she read a story, the book upside down for her, and paused frequently to ask a question of a child, such as 'You have a pink dress like this haven't you Mary?' or 'Peter, what did Topsy say to Tim?', and she was 'interrupted' by the children making comments which were often not related to the story. Perhaps the story or a word had sparked off another flash of thought or an association of ideas, or perhaps the limits of a child's concentration span had been reached.

But the overall effect was one of communication and use of

language, in which the story was largely a catalyst rather than necessarily a conveyor, and the interruptions were not in fact interruptions, but reactions and participation. In the classroom or the library this is all part of the teaching and learning process.

The average librarian is probably accustomed to a receptive, usually obedient and captivated audience, hopefully controllable by a look or a quiet word, or by invitation to participate, listening to a story from beginning to end, with unconscious visible and audible reactions rather than interruptions. To the librarian with that kind of experience, the teacher's method seems fragmented and possibly destructive of the storyflow.

But there are different purposes for storytelling, different methods and tellers, and different stories can be chosen to elicit particular responses. Given the effect of mental handicap on brain performance and responsiveness and on social experience, it is only to be expected that one story can produce a variety of responses. This happens with the ordinary child listening to a story, but the irrelevant response is usually quickly suppressed, either from social/educational conditioning or because that reaction has been superseded by a relevant response as the story progresses.

The teller of stories to children with visual, hearing or mental disabilities must be prepared for some extraordinary reactions, including delay in the speed of reaction, the display of aural and physical responses, the need to ask questions or to make comments, and the possibility, in a few listeners, of lack of comprehension leading probably to inattention and subsequent distracted and distracting behaviour – even with the most carefully chosen story.

The mentally handicapped child has a literal mind, so stories with puns, abstract ideas and language, metaphors and possibly those set in a fairy world or unfamiliar background, need to be avoided. It helps if the following features are present:

1 Just one concept per episode or story.
2 Not too many characters, and those should have simple names.
3 Clear actions, logical in cause and effect.
4 Dialogue, if it is in understandable vocabulary.

5 Little description and that should be very clear.
6 A beginning, a middle and an end.
7 Themes such as nature, the family, daily life, shopping, holidays, school, traffic, emotions.
8 Possibilities for voice/sound effects to aid comprehension and provide participation, e.g. animal and train sounds.
9 Repetition of words or phrases to reinforce learning and comprehension, and to provide opportunity for response and participation.
10 Humour; situation humour rather than puns, which require a knowledge of what is normal in order to appreciate what is humorously abnormal.
11 A happy ending.

I have read and told stories to mentally handicapped children in institutions, including a child of nine in a special care unit. She was grossly handicapped, mentally and physically; she had multiple deformities and was unable to move any part of her body except her eyes, and she was unable to communicate.

She spent all day on a water bed, which the nurses touched every time they passed in order to give her some movement, and above her were mobiles, posters and streamers to give some visual interest, if she could see. On five consecutive weeks I spent ten minutes with her, holding picture books above her eyes and talking about them and the story to her. There was no response until the fourth and fifth occasions, when her eyes flickered and brightened. It was, is, impossible to tell whether the response was the result of recognizing me either by sight, smell or sound, or recognizing the picture books, or indeed whether the response was of pleasure or displeasure. The nurses were pleased that some stimulus had been offered, even though there was little evidence that it had been received. The fact that the girl would certainly die within about two years was not significant in terms of whether or not she should be helped to gain pleasure, nor was the lack of evidence that any such gain had taken place, significant. If favourable response were a requirement to justify continuation, much of what is undertaken in the name of education would be stopped very soon.

A colleague spent three years telling stories weekly to a class of mentally handicapped eighteen- and nineteen-year-old boys and girls. All found it very rewarding and enjoyable to share the picture books normally associated with young children; *Where is the Green Parrot?* *Harry the Dirty Dog* and *The Three Bears* being typical of the most enjoyed stories and of the kind of content. In the first, repetition, visual discrimination in searching for the parrot, and incongruity in finding the parrot where it was not expected, produced responses ranging from mild amusement to paroxysms of laughter. *Harry* was obviously identified with as a proxy boy who did 'naughty' things, though some equated him with dogs in their own families. *The Three Bears* involved identification with the inside of a house and familiar objects like chair, table, bowl, bed and the possessiveness many children show towards 'their' property. Repetition, fear and retribution were also attractive features, possibly conditioned by the behaviour modification efforts they must all have experienced!

Groups of children brought to the public library normally need their own storytime so that the story and the children's need and ability can be matched and response time allowed.

The librarian with children in the classroom or school library soon learns what satisfies and helps the children, both collectively and individually, and can tailor the time, the story and the follow-up to the known group. This is done by Patricia Scott, in Tasmania, who receives a special grant from the Schools Commission to tell stories regularly to children in several special schools in the Hobart area, evidence that at least one authority is convinced of the value of stories.

Storytelling and the hearing impaired child

A child with hearing impairment needs all the help he can get to enjoy and benefit from story sessions, and attention should be paid to the following points:

1 Explanation should be given beforehand of the salient features of the story. 'This story is about . . .' Such an introduction needs careful preparation or it may mislead the child, confuse him or give away a vital punchline.
2 The book, visual aids and objects to be used with the story should be shown to the children before beginning.

   This introduction enables the child to know what key words he is looking for in lipreading or listening for via his hearing-aid, and it ensures that if there is a change of subject, or if a new character appears in the course of the story, he is prepared for the changes.

Such an introduction also provides the child with the opportunity to accommodate himself to the storyteller's personal speech and facial idiosyncrasies, both of which can affect the comprehension of the hearing impaired child. In addition, he may need to adjust his hearing aid, move his position to a place better for seeing or hearing, and generally get himself ready for the anticipated enjoyment.

3 The choice of story is crucial, and it should incorporate the following:

(a) Action language and overt mood rather than building it up by description and subtle language or interwoven into the plot.

(b) Simple sentence structure and vocabulary, and repetition.

(c) Familiar or identifiable themes. Fairy stories are often not usable until three or more years *after* they might be used with hearing children, despite the economy of plot in most of them, because the language is often strange and difficult.

(d) A single concept in the one story to enable the child to relax in the knowledge that *that* is what the story is about.

(e) Stories which help to increase knowledge and skill in social aspects.

(f) Books with clear pictures which can help the child to identify the subject, the character and the vocabulary.

4 The storyteller's methods need particular emphasis on bodily and facial expression to convey visually what might normally be conveyed by tone of voice in a sharp or angry word, by the use of a slow hushed tone to create suspense or by the use of increased tempo to create excitement. Tone and speed are not vehicles for good communication with the hearing impaired child, a difficult adaptation to make for the storyteller used to relying heavily on the voice with hearing children.

5 Other visual information can be supplied in the form of pictures, toys, and objects and time must be allowed for the child to look away from the lips and to take in the picture or object. It is, again, difficult for a storyteller to remember

not to speak when he wants the child's attention on the picture or object. The child cannot look at the picture and the lips at the same time, and he needs the visuals to *see* in support of what he hopes, or thinks, he has heard.

6 It is useful to take the story slowly and to pause from time to time to enable children to both comprehend and react. Although I have normal hearing, I can appreciate the difficulty of the deaf listener through my extensive experience of trying to cope with simultaneous translation. While I am able to see the 'live' speaker, a translator's voice comes over the headphones seconds behind what can be seen on the live speaker's lips and, of course, differently. The time-lag means that the section of the audience who understand the live speaker react to what he is saying immediately, the rest of us react seconds later, if at all. For the deaf child, the time-lag in comprehension means that he misses the next part of the story if the teller goes too fast. A pause now and again, means that his mind can digest what has been said, rather than continually having to work hard to 'hear' what is said.

It may be necessary to repeat or paraphrase if there is evidence that the children have not understood.

7 The storyteller must ensure that his face is towards the light or is spotlit; that no mannerisms or other things obscure the mouth; that all the children can see both storyteller and book or other visual aids; that the programme is short or broken up into short sections, so that the very tiring effort of intensive lipreading or concentrated listening can be coped with; that the equipment needed for hearing-aid loops, overhead projectors, whiteboards, etc, is to hand and working; and that an interpreter in the form of a signer, for instance, is available if necessary, to 'tell' the story along with the speaking storyteller.

Most hearing impaired children are intelligent, and though frustrated by difficulties in hearing, speaking and usually retarded reading, they find release in the story told.

Storytelling and the visually handicapped child

Storytelling for visually handicapped children requires different adaptations, relying more on the quality of the story to present in descriptive terms what might otherwise be understood in visual terms, and requiring the storyteller to practice verbal intonation to convey what might otherwise be conveyed by facial expression. Particular factors that the storyteller should be aware of are:

1. Can the story stand on its own without illustration, does it have clear description and detail?
2. Does it lend itself to vocal expression, i.e. change of voice for different characters, and varying inflexions of tone to represent conflicting emotions, such as anger, pleasure, happiness or sadness?
3. As with some mentally handicapped children, the concepts of size and shape may be underdeveloped, so stories relying on these as a basic concept should be avoided unless the description is very clear.
4. The use of objects mentioned in the story is always a possibility, whether for ordinary or special children, but whereas the object may not be in accord with the sighted child's mental image stimulated by the words, for the visually handicapped child the object may actually provide an image which would otherwise have been non-existent or faulty. So stories that involve senses other than sight, such as smell, taste, touch, number, and, of course, the sense of fun, are usually enjoyable.
5. Response may be delayed, as in the deaf child, since comprehension relies mainly on one sense, in this case hearing, with touch as a second line conveyor of information, so time must be allowed for this delay.
6. The visible response which storytellers rely on to control or adapt their telling, may not be forthcoming. Catching the eye of a child, seeing excitement or fear on his face, and noting the inattention of wandering eyes, are all aspects of interaction which the storyteller/teacher/lecturer consciously or unconsciously notices and uses, but such clues to reaction may not be present in the the blind or partially sighted child, and the storyteller learns instead to take note of body movement and audible reaction from his visually impaired audience.

As with the deaf child, the constraints on reading fluently can cause the visually handicapped child to find it hard work, so that the right story, taken from the printed page, creates a freely enjoyable, heard, experience.

Non-fiction

The use of non-fiction in book sessions and storytimes, is an important factor in attracting and gaining the attention of many children, particularly boys.

The mentally handicapped child who perhaps cannot appreciate a story, is often fascinated by fact, and many librarians show a range of information books on themes of known interest to the group or individual, either because the information books complement aspects studied in school or because their themes are identifiable as personal interests.

My own experience shows that books on animals and pets, gardening and sport are popular, and that many mentally handicapped teenage girls avidly 'read' books on grooming and personal relationships and many boys are very interested in motor bikes and cars though they may not, or never will, be able to drive either.

In all cases, the choice of information books for use in story/book time requires the presenter to analyse not only what can be presented at such a time, but whether what is attractive and informative then, is also comprehensible when, appetite whetted, the child subsequently wants to read it, with or without adult help. Much of my 'learning by experience' in this matter was by trial and error, initially with subnormal young teenage boys, educationally subnormal rather than mentally, though some were near the border line. These boys, able to read with difficulty, if at all, but of near normal intelligence, were turned off print and were therefore in a hostile mood, when assembled for the initial book-talk. By a varied programme of facts of the 'did-you-know-that . . .?' variety, stories and extracts read and told, information book snippets, and carefully selected, appetite-whetting, bits from cassette books, the mood changed. After that first session many asked to borrow the information books concerned. There was, however, a distinct gap between what they could understand when I read and interpreted, and directed their attention to these books, and what they could cope with on their own. This led me to look again at what I chose for such presentations and to make my own distinction between the information books that could be used by the children on their own and those that required adult assistance. For older children there is a dearth of the former.

However, as many handicapped children have adult or peer group help at school, though fewer have it at home, it is possible by this means to aid and inform the teachers who accompany the children, on the range of information books containing features suitable for the children in their care.

Most handicapped children have difficulty with reading and such difficulty usually precludes pleasure in reading, but many information books are 'easier' to read than fiction. As there are a greater number of handicapped boys than girls, and research shows that 'normal' boys read more non-fiction than girls, it makes sense to promote information books as a source of pleasure and information, and to whet the appetite with 'tasters' at book sessions and 'storytimes'. Materials useful for storytelling or storyreading include:

1. Stories on tape and film.
2. Filmstrip and tape, e.g. Weston Woods.
3. Pictures from magazines or discarded books to back up pictureless stories.
4. Flannelgraphs.
5. Boards.
6. Puppets.
7. Objects.
8. Pop-up books.
9. Scratch and sniff books.
10. Music.
11. Sound effects on tape.
12. Songs, e.g. Gadsby, D and Harrop, B. *Okki-tokki-unga.*

Volunteer storytellers are also needed. Librarians and teachers, on the whole, do not have time to carry out all the storytelling needed for the children in their community or school and will often welcome volunteers for public library, hospital or school sessions.

Librarians and teachers do not have a monopoly of storytelling skills, but others may need to be briefed on the special aspects of story selection, delivery and follow-up, as already discussed.

As an example of one person's methods, I describe my own in detail in connection with one particular story, *The Elephant and the Bad Baby*[1] which, with variations for the deaf, blind and mentally handicapped, contains most of the elements needed for all three groups. After indicating the nature of the story, I name the characters and give the children character-name cards, and show them the pictures, superbly created by Raymond Briggs, so that all will know what an elephant looks like (since it is likely to be unfamiliar) and all will recognize the probably familiar shopkeepers and foods in the story. For the visually handicapped children, I assign the names verbally to individual children and offer a model elephant for tactile information. Then I ask the children to say 'please', a crucial word in the story, after which we practice the word 'rumpeta'; both words are on the board or on cards for visual reinforcement. Then I tell the story with the children joining in with 'rumpeta rumpeta' in more or less appropriate places. After that, with many groups, I am able to dramatize the story, getting some children to 'be' the characters and to do the actions, while others hold up cards with the key words 'apple', 'ice cream' etc, and I tell the story again. In some cases the children are able to, and wish to say the dialogue bits themselves.

Not only is this a story useful for social training in saying please and thank you, and in identifying shops and their wares, but it positively forces even speech handicapped children to join in as the elephant goes 'rumpeta rumpeta' down the street with the bad baby on its back. It allows the child to feel superior, because *he* would have said please, and it provides a certain amount of controlled participation and activity.

There are a great many books available on storytelling and a great many lists of stories to tell, and some recommendations for these are given at the end of this chapter. But if storytellers test potential stories against the criteria indicated here and then match the results with the needs and abilities of the child or group of handicapped children to whom they tell stories, a personal list will grow. And it is the storyteller's personal liking for a story that can often make the difference between the child who has simply understood the story and the child who has lost himself in it.

Select list of books about storytelling and of stories to tell:

Baker, Augusta and Greene, Ellis. *Storytelling: art and technique.* New York: Bowker, 1978.

Bellon, Elmer C. Language development through storytelling activities: a theoretical base and techniques for language development. *School Media Quarterly*, no. 3, Winter 1975, pp. 149–56.

Library Association, Youth Libraries Group. *Storytelling: practical guides series, collection of papers on aspects of storytelling and reading, by experienced storytellers.* London: LA, Youth Libraries Group, 1979.

Sawyer, Ruth. *The Way of the Storyteller.* London: Bodley Head, 1968.

Smith, Eve. *Some Aspects of Storytelling in Second Language Teaching.* London: Commission for Racial Equality, 1974. (This covers the problems of colloquial language and structure which confuse the second language learner, and thus may be useful for the problems of the deaf or non-English speaking handicapped child.)

Colwell, Eileen. *Humblepuppy.* London: Bodley Head, 1978.

Hallworth, Grace and Marriage, Julia. *Stories to Read and to Tell.* London: LA, Youth Libraries Group, 1978. (An annotated list.)

Chapter Eleven

Stock selection for the handicapped child

STOCK SELECTION requires the librarian to assess material from the simplest to the most complex, textually and visually in print, aurally and visually in film and audio material, and intellectually and emotionally in all media. This is no less true when selecting for the special child, indeed the judgement is even more crucial.

It may be that categorizing books as suitable for one or other of the handicaps would provide the reader with a ready-made check for a specific handicap, but as many of the requirements overlap between the handicaps and as many children have more than one handicap, the criteria are given as generally appropriate, though due emphasis is made when there is an aspect special to a particular handicap. This section is not concerned with the selection of material for classroom use, only that which is for inclusion in the library.

No attempt is made to indicate the selection criteria for ordinary children's books and periodicals, either fiction or non-fiction, as these are well documented elsewhere, and it is assumed that such knowledge is already possessed by a librarian. Only those factors which pertain particularly to the reading needs of the special child in terms of physical, visual or mental ability and need, are considered.

Stock selection is frequently better carried out as a team effort, whether at selection meetings or by co-operation with others, and for those who are selecting for the complete range of age and ability, it pays to view all material with 'special' needs in mind.

New materials, seen in library suppliers, bookshops, on approval from the supplier, in exhibition collections, in central purchase collections, educational publishing houses and teachers' centres, and noticed in catalogues, bibliographies and reviews, need to be assessed for special features. It helps if special school and regular school staff and librarians examine 'approval' and exhibition collections; if local public library and school library staff co-operate; if teachers and librarians, and hospital library and medical staff are encouraged to recommend additions to stock; and if a regular moderating process is instituted to assess how useful these special items are, once selected.

It helps if at least once a year all those locally concerned with the special child meet to discuss the selection of materials, as happened recently in Herefordshire, England, when the Director of the Public Library arranged for schools, organizations, the schools library service and children's libraries to discuss library provision for the special child. For there is often a lack of knowledge of the special requirements on the part of many teachers and librarians who work with handicapped children. They may discover, in time and by experience, which are the materials suited to their children, and most bemoan the dearth of appropriate books. It makes sense, therefore, to look at the requirements in order to be better able to identify them when and where possible, whether in special material or from amongst the vast range of ordinary children's books.

The quantity to be selected is related to the nature and number of children served and is recommended in the various standards for school and public library stock selection. Such standards apply equally to libraries for special children as to those for ordinary children, as exemplified in the British school library recommended guidelines for school library resource centres[1] and the American Library Association *Standards for Library Services for the Blind and Visually Handicapped*,[2] both of which specify ten books per child up to the age of fifteen.

However, there is often a discrepancy between standards and practice which is further complicated by the apparent dearth of suitable material to meet the criteria. The kinds of material to be selected for libraries serving special children include:

1 Ordinary children's and adult books, fiction and non-fiction, hardback and paperback.
2 Books for reading retarded children and young adults.
3 Picture books.

4 Large print books and braille material.
5 Non-traditional materials, e.g. tactual books, pop-up, scratch and sniff, raised surface, rag books, etc.
6 Cassettes, tapes, discs.
7 Film material.
8 Simplified and adapted editions, e.g. for the deaf.
9 Kits and sets of material.
10 Charts and pictures.
11 Careers material.
12 Toys and games.
13 Periodicals.
14 Journals and newsletters of societies for the handicapped and of special educational bodies.
15 Catalogues of national library services for the handicapped.
16 Information for files of relevant local and national organizations and individuals.
17 Trade catalogues of equipment, etc, for the handicapped.
18 Information on radio/TV programmes for and about handicapped children.
19 Books for parents and others about the handicapped child.
20 Anthologies of stories for storytelling.

There are many normal children's books which contain the features needed. The content, structure and illustration of some of these need further analysis to indicate the special requirements.

Content

1 Perception. Mentally handicapped, hearing impaired, visually handicapped and some physically handicapped children, share a common effect of their disabilities, and this is difficulty in comprehending aspects like colour, number, size, time, speed and weight, which the average child with all his senses often understands by unconscious aural and visual assimilation, aided by normal experience and by school education.

Though the causes of this difficulty vary from mental inability through language and sight defects, to physical disability, the effect is the same. Colour, shape and size discrimination are learned by experience and by training involving matching, sorting and grading exercises, which in turn use skills of vision, touch, taste, smell, hearing and perception.

Where these things are incorporated into books to be either used by the children or *with* the children, then the books become another medium of experience and instruction to complement and supplement, or perhaps compensate for, the lack of experience of the child.

Examples of perception developers include Henry Pluckrose's *Things Big and Small*, *Things Left and Right*, *Things Light and Heavy*, *Things that Pull*, *Things to Touch* (published by Franklin Watts), using specially taken photographs and carefully devised text.

Similarly, Tana Hoban's books *Push and Pull*, *Shapes and Things*, *Count and See* cover concepts of weight, size and number using the left hand page for the simple text, and the right hand page for clear black and white photographs of known objects.

But these concepts of colour, number, size, time, speed and weight have practical aspects too, and can be treated by authors and illustrators in differing ways, not all of which are suitable for the special child. One crucial difference lies in the objects shown in the illustrations. Handicapped children tend to have a limited experience in a limited environment and may have difficulty making sense of what they are able to see or hear, so all who work with handicapped children stress the need to select books which apply the concepts mentioned to known everyday objects or events.

Though there are numerous alphabet and counting books on the market, there is a difference between, say, Brian Wildsmith's *ABC* with its 'I for Iguana' and John Burningham's *ABC* with 'I for Ice cream'. There is a difference between William Stobbs' counting book *Gaping Widemouthed Waddling Frog* where there are 'monkeys tied to a clog' and Dick Bruna's *I Can Count* where the things to be counted are familiar.

There is a difference too, in the style of illustration, though the first examples in each case are no doubt worthy for ordinary children, the second examples in each case contain clear, unambiguous, identifiable pictures of known things.

2 To aid the development of understanding 'doing' words and the names of things, it is important to look for books which contain action verbs and noun labels – again in a familiar setting. Dick Bruna's *I Can Read* names parts of the body, Anne

Rockwell's *The Toolbox* names the tools. *I Spy*, a picture book of objects in a child's home environment, by Lucille Ogle and Tina Thoburn, is designed to encourage recognition and stimulate language, as does Inger and Lasse Sandberg's *Daniel's Helping Hand*, Gunille Wolde's *Thomas Goes To The Doctor* and Dean Hay's *Things in the Kitchen.*

3 Relevance to the child's experience includes topics such as domestic animals, the home, school, hospital, transport, toys and people, and there are many children's books on these themes. But fantasy and unknown settings can be unhelpful, if not incomprehensible, to many deaf and mentally handicapped children; the former because of language deficiency, where words have been acquired the hard way and tend to relate to the immediate and necessary aspects of life and where the meanings of words are better understood if the things they relate to can be seen; the latter because of a mental inability to perceive *this* world clearly and a tendency towards a literal belief.

Relevance to the known environment is one aspect, another is relevance to the experienced fears and emotions. All children can identify to varying degrees, the mentally handicapped child relating particularly to stories involving love, family or group life, fear of the unknown and of punishment, thus *Harry the Dirty Dog* is well liked, as are Roger Hargreaves' *Mr* books and Judith Kerr's *The Tiger Who Came to Tea.*

4 The more able mentally handicapped teenager is pleased to find subject content relevant to his chronological age, for though his mental age is lower, he lives in a world in which he sees teenagers, and, unless hospitalized, probably lives with or meets teenagers.

Few special editions of non-fiction suitable for older children are produced, but some British examples include series like:

Read Your Way (Cassell)
Blackwell's Learning Library
First Look At (Franklin Watts)
Inner Ring Sports, Facts and True Stories Series (Benn)
Macdonald's Easy Reading Series, including Visual Books, Countries, Introduction to Nature

and the many materials listed in the Library Association's adult recommendations (Margaret Redfern, (ed.) *New Readers Start Here*. London: LA, 1975).

Ordinary non-fiction series containing the appropriate features include:

Blackwell's Looking at . . . Series
Macmillan Educational, What Do They Do Series
Hamish Hamilton, Star Book Series
Nelson, Lively Reader Series
Muller, Junior True Book Series
A & C Black, Young Mathematician Series
A & C Black, Let's Look Series
Worlds Work, Children's University Series

In every commercial venture much is conditioned by potential sales. The number of hearing impaired children is small in market terms, but the 'simple' editions are now known to be very helpful for all reading disabled children whatever the cause, and this, though it embraces an all too large number of children and young people, makes a 'simple' edition a viable commercial proposition, especially so in a country where the mother tongue is also an internationally used language.

There are many ordinary information books which contain the means to inform visually. For instance, the first criterion is that the illustrative content be relevant to both the topic of the book and of the page, and relevant to the reader's need and/or experience. Single topic pictures are always appropriate for the mentally handicapped child and for many hearing impaired children, and all reading retarded children benefit from illustrations which relate to the text, which depict exactly what the text states and which are not distracting in the quantity of extraneous background, embellishment or abstract design.

The use of colour, either in illustration or photography, adds information normally taken for granted because it tends to be unconsciously assimilated. Colour enables objects and people to be better identified. But black and white illustrations are acceptable if they clearly delineate the matter depicted. Visually and mentally handicapped children need to have clear outlines in order to discern the relevant and to have neither the mind nor the eye distracted. A random glance at many information books reveals the difference between those books in which the pictures objectively inform visually, and those in which the pictures are merely decoration for the topic; between those in which the illustrations or photographs are crammed with detail, which is likely to confuse the handicapped reader who cannot extract the relevant from a mass of undifferentiated information, and those in which the illustration or photograph concentrates on the salient features of the topic. The suitability of the illustrative content is seen in its most controversial context in books on sex education.

Some mentally handicapped young people who have a teenager's physical development are as interested in the opposite sex as the normal teenager, but less able to handle their feelings or actions. This is discussed in the chapter on the mentally handicapped child, but simple books on sex and reproduction are needed by many reading retarded children whatever their disability. An excellent select list of materials on sex education is Janet Newman's *Sex Education: a critical evaluation of materials* (YLG pamphlet no. 20. London: LA, Youth Libraries Group, 1979) in which the annotations refer to many of the aspects which make or mar the treatment of this subject, including the common error of misleading illustrations, misleading to the ordinary child, but particularly so to the mentally handicapped.

Relevance of any non-fiction content to the child depends upon his use of library non-fiction or information books for school work and for personal leisure purposes. However, the features needed to ensure that the factual content is understood and usable are worthy of consideration by the selector, as are the structural features.

Structure

The handicapped child who has difficulty in reading because of language deficiency caused by deafness, who is slow to read because of sight defects, who has a mental deficiency, or who is reading retarded, needs to be aided towards comprehension by the structure of the story or information content. Thus the relevant criteria for selection include the presence of the following features in the book under assessment:

1 A definite beginning and ending. The hearing impaired child

needs aurally or visually to know the start and finish and the scope in his everyday conversations or lessons and also needs help in this way with books. The mentally handicapped child and others who are easily distracted are given an aid to concentration by a clear start and finish, and where there is a mental inability to deduce or imagine an ending it is necessary to tie up the ends beyond doubt.

2 Simple descriptive vocabulary and dialogue. The simplicity is needed because most handicapped children are reading retarded; the hearing impaired child is often short of word knowledge and the mentally handicapped child unable to identify difficult or strange words.

The description lies not in the lengthy 'purple' passages in many normal books for children and adults, but in the use of appropriate and rich-in-meaning words and phrases. The visually handicapped child may also benefit from a text which describes, and, unless severely deficient in vision, may, in the case of picture books, be able to use the pictures to reinforce the descriptive text.

Simple dialogue is useful for the deaf child to *see* the spoken conversational word, and if the writer is good at producing dialogue he will have caught the inflexion and tone of voice accurately, which in turn aids the child reader, or adult reading to the child, adding another source of recognition and identification, and thus reinforcing the meaning conveyed by the written word.

3 Repetition. This provides a number of aids for the child. It stamps the word or phrase in the memory. It reinforces the memory of the word in context and later, hopefully, depending upon the word, out of context. It provides continuity in the story or information book, and it enables the child to feel the pleasure of recognition and thus gives a comfortable feeling of familiarity.

The constant repetition of names where otherwise 'he' or 'she' might have been used may help to 'set' a character for those who cannot equate a 'he' or 'she' with the person to whom it refers. Some visually handicapped and deaf children are accustomed to the use of proper names in this way to aid identification in everyday life and some mentally handicapped children have difficulty with anything less than clear concrete terms and names. The deliberate repetition of words and phrases to encourage vocal participation is also an asset, and is found in many stories for children.

Repetition in information books is vital, preferably in words and pictures. While recapitulation is standard practice in normal teaching, it needs to be more consciously done for many mentally handicapped and learning disabled children, in both teaching and reading material. The old saying about public speaking – 'Tell them what you are going to tell them, tell them, and then tell them what you have told them' is vital in information books for the less able.

4 One concept, theme or episode. This aspect is of more concern to the mentally handicapped child who is unable to grasp more than one idea at a time, or to unravel an interwoven or parallel plot, and for the deaf child who, as in a conversation, gets lost if the subject switches without adequate warning to another topic. The visually handicapped child may have little visual information to aid him and thus needs to concentrate on the main theme. Other learning disabled children also benefit in that the mind can concentrate on the theme without other ideas or information to distract attention, thus a smoother flow of thought and comprehension can occur.

Whereas the able reader can note and assimilate information additional to or decorating the theme, the less able child may not be able to select what is relevant from a mass of information.

Thus the Breakthrough adaptation of *Topsy and Tim at School* has all the merits discussed so far, plus the concentration on the day's activities in school. Similarly, the Macdonald Starters Series, e.g. *Rain*, and the Franklin Watts First Look At Series, e.g. *A First Look at Telephones*, contain most of the features to satisfy the criteria so far.

For the older child, Lois Lenski's *Papa Small* depicts the daily round and common tasks of the Small family in attractively described and illustrated style, using concepts, objects and activities with the main theme of family life. The Macdonald First Library Series and the Ladybird Easy Reading People at Work Series, both with a book on *the Policeman*, are also useful examples of one-topic books with a high interest, low vocabulary content.

5 No word play, metaphors or foreign words. Many handicapped children have difficulty with everyday language and are thus at a disadvantage if faced with words from another language.

Metaphor is defined by the Oxford English Dictionary as 'a figure of speech in which a name or descriptive term is transferred to some object different from, but analogous to, that to which it is properly applicable'. So the mental process requires a mind which can both understand the original name or term and the borrowed one or analogous one. Such imagery is confusing for those handicapped children who take things literally and for the language deficient child.

Word play and verbal puns again only work if the reader understands the normal usage of words. In most areas of life the abnormal can only be recognized if the normal is known. In the context of children's books this applies only to words and is not to be confused with appreciation of incongruity in the action. For example, many mentally handicapped children have the *Mr* books (which in fact match all the criteria) and find the incongruity of the opening page of *Mr Funny* very amusing:

> Mr Funny lived in a teapot!
> It had two bedrooms, a bathroom, a kitchen and a living-room and it suited Mr Funny very nicely.

Similarly, in W. Zacherias' *Where is the Green Parrot?* the children are amused at the unusual, incongruous, abnormal places in which the green parrot is found. Such incongruity is acceptable when set in a background that is known to the children.

6 Appropriate length of sentence, chapter, book. Many teaching schemes, early reading books and adult literacy reading material follow the rule of starting each sentence on a new line. This helps the reader who has difficulty with the linear approach needed for reading, and complements the full stop or period. It also breaks up the page into a less daunting layout than a block of continuous print, thus providing both greater psychological appeal and probably greater visual legibility.

The length of the sentence affects comprehension in that the longer it is, the more likely it is to contain clauses and sub-clauses (possibly parentheses also) covering a number of ideas rather than a single theme; and the more difficult it is for the reader to maintain concentration and to hold in mind the original idea, indicated at the beginning of the sentence. This last sentence was written to exemplify the problem and if it were re-written to fit the need for short sentences it would appear as follows:

The length of a sentence affects comprehension.
The longer it is the more likely it is to contain clauses and sub-clauses.
(It may include parentheses also).
A long sentence is likely to cover a number of ideas rather than a single theme.
This makes it more difficult for the reader to maintain concentration.
It makes it more difficult for him to hold in mind the original idea indicated at the beginning of the long sentence.

The length of the chapter also affects concentration. Chapters are usually found in fiction and non-fiction books for older readers, and are devices for separating ideas or episodes or stages of knowledge, thus a chapter may be useful for the handicapped child who needs clear demarcation between one aspect and another or one stage of plot and another. But chapters need to be short to avoid the necessity for lengthy concentration, and to narrow the treatment of the ideas to assimilable portions. It is not necessary with the more able children to reduce the *range or depth* of coverage, simply to break it up into more steps, so that the reader can progress a step at a time.

It helps if each chapter is self-contained, without the need to refer to previous or coming chapters, though reinforcement and repetition throughout are useful.

7 A high interest, low vocabulary content. The style of writing suitable for the reading retarded child with whatever other disability, revolves round the necessity for high interest and low

vocabulary, and there are an increasing number of such publications in several countries.

The books tend to be set in realistic and relevant situations in order to aid comprehension. Reading involves not only identifying the letters and the words as pronounceable, but defining the meaning of the word in the dictionary sense, determining the meaning given to the word by the author within the context, and assigning the meaning which the reader's own experience has given to the word. The more familiar the reader is with situations described by the word, the better he understands the text.

The easier it is to find meaning in what is read, the more motivated the reader is to do it again, thus gaining practice and increasing skill. Abstract ideas often require greater sentence length and more difficult words, so most books designed for the reading retarded tend to be descriptive and situational rather than analytical.

There are many simplified and adapted editions of books for children and though some of these were mentioned in the chapter on the hearing impaired child, they are repeated here. British examples of fiction include:

(a) Breakthrough Trust. Home Library: simple language editions of books for children. 20 titles adapted from ordinary editions of books for young children.
(b) British Association of Teachers of the Deaf. Adaptations of books, e.g. the Ladybird book *Scott of the Antarctic.*
(c) Oxford University Press. Pictorial Classics.
(d) Blackie. Kennet Library: Modern series (popular stories).
(e) Blackie. Phoenix Library: Classics.
(f) Hutchinson Educational. Bullseye Books (adaptations of best sellers).
(g) Longman. Structured Readers (popular titles).
(h) Longman. Simplified English series (2000 word vocabulary).
(i) Longman. Bridge series (3000 word vocabulary, e.g. *Lucky Jim*, *The Invisible Man*).
(j) Heinemann. Guided Readers (Fiction and non-fiction).

The first three in the list are the simplest and are suitable for younger children, while the rest are of interest to those with a ten plus mental age and eleven plus interest age.

The problem of lack of sufficient material suitable for reading retarded teenagers, particularly the mentally handicapped teenager (and the adults they grow into), is alleviated in some countries by the use of much pictorial literature including photographic books, tourist guides, charts, and audio-visual material, both story and informational. To these can be added the many British books for teenage, less able readers, particularly series like the Trigger (Collins), Forward (Methuen), Manxman (Dent), Onward (Cassell), Breakthrough (Penguin), Checkers (Evans), Club 75 (Macmillan), Crown Street Kings (Macmillan), Inner Ring (Benn), Inswinger (Hulton Ed.), Solos (Hart Davis) and Joan Tate Books (Heinemann).

Cassell Educational produces several series: Disco Books for reading age six to seven and interest age fifteen to sixteen; Club Books for reading age six and a half to seven and a half and interest age fourteen to sixteen; Banjo Books for reading age seven to eight and interest age ten to fourteen; and Anchor Books for reading age eight and a half to nine and interest age ten to fourteen.

These, and the extensive Trend series (Cheshire/Ginn), offer teenage interest themes in graded vocabulary. The value of these books lies in the high interest, low vocabulary content, the slightly bigger print, the layout involving more white space than average and the quantity of illustration, which gives both visual clues to the text and an attractive appearance. These, plus the paperback format, offer reading retarded teenagers the possibility of success in reading after failure with conventional books.

8 Illustrations in books and periodicals. Some mention has already been made of this but it is useful to list here the factors already mentioned throughout the book. Illustrations should be:

(a) representational rather than abstract.
(b) colour rather than black and white, whether illustrations or photographs.
(c) strictly related to the text.
(d) relevant to the life of the reader (where appropriate).

(e) single object, or clearly defined pictures, framed rather than 'bled' to the edge of the page, by means of frames or circles, or 'contained' by a lot of white space.
(f) uncluttered by overprinted text.

In picture books it is helpful if the text runs consistently along the top or foot of the page rather than anywhere and everywhere, to assist the visual linear sequence and continuity.

Where possible it is helpful to have the illustration on the right hand page and text on the left hand page as the automatic reaction of the reader is look first at the right hand page. A possible explanation for this is that this page is visible when the new left hand is obscured while the page is being turned. Whatever the reason, the child benefits from looking for visual clues in the picture to aid him with the text.

Physical aspects of the book

Certain aspects should be considered in selecting books for the handicapped child, either because they aid the child, or are economy factors for the selector.

1 Weight and size. Paperbacks can be an economy in the sense of being able to buy several for the price of one hardback, and in the particular interest they hold for the more able teenage reader. Given the small print and the reading ability required, they are suitable for some of the physically handicapped who have difficulty with the size and weight of the hardback, and for the able readers amongst the handicapped.

At the other end of the scale the large print and Braille books are normally of a size requiring special space in shelving and table use, as are large picture books for young children. The large size of many newspapers and periodicals also requires recognition of the need for space and equipment to read comfortably.

2 Print size. As indicated in the chapter on the visually handicapped, legibility of print needs the selector's attention, bearing in mind that 12 point is the normal print size, and that 14 point upwards is likely to be useful for increased legibility to aid the reading retarded and the visually handicapped. But print size alone is inadequate, and must be accompanied by a suitably clear type face, good leading (space between the lines), extra weight

of print i.e. blacker ink and/or thicker strokes, and non-glare paper. Spaces between letters, between words and in excess between lines, will not always improve legibility, but will probably improve motivation. Lists of books with such features are cited in the visually handicapped chapter.

3 Strength. Many books receive rough treatment by partially sighted children who perhaps lean heavily on the book, which is flat on the table, in order to bring the eyes near to the page, or who must force the book's binding to lie flat on a reading stand. Mentally handicapped children may not have the manual delicacy required for handling pages or books or may use the book as an object for activity in addition to reading. The physically handicapped child may not have the fine motor co-ordination needed for careful handling of books.

I tested a few rag and board books in a hospital school for severely mentally handicapped children and the books lasted between three and six months in those extreme conditions. Some of these are mentioned later in this chapter, in the section on unusual material.

4 Visual appeal. The initial choice of a book by a child is directly related to the external visual appeal of the cover. This is so for all children and is then followed by an unconscious assessment of the visual appeal of the illustrative content, colour having an obvious impact, the page layout and the appearance of the text, both in quantity and legibility. Then comes the visual appeal of the illustrative content in terms of relevance to experience, and, finally, relevance to need.

So the selector must judge the visual appeal in relation to the child as a reader and then the particular appeal relevant to the handicap.

Unusual material

There is a large amount of visual and print material which is not normally considered as suitable for selection by librarians, partly because of the physical format which makes library handling difficult, and child handling expensive, and partly because the quality of the content of much of this material may be deemed less than literary in normal critical terms.

However, much of this material has something to offer the

child unable to cope with print or visual information presented in the usual way, and who needs additional stimuli. For this reason many teachers and librarians of the handicapped do look for unusual material to complement and supplement the more traditional library stock. Such material can include:

Tactile/raised surface/plasticized/twin vision materials.
Scratch and sniff books.
Pop-up books.
Mirror and overlay books.
Rag or cloth books.
Board (stiff card pages) books.
Concertina strips.
Laminated pictures.
Kits, games and toys (adapted for the blind, e.g. chess, beetle, cards, dominoes).
Deaf sign language playing cards.
Charts for communication and step-by-step instruction.
Comics and magazines.
Tapes and discs.
Music.
Film material (e.g. slides).
Toys.

1 Examples of tactile and twin vision books are given in the chapter on the visually handicapped, but *What's That?* by Virginia Allan Jensen and Dorcas Woodbury Haller is suitable for many other children.

Designed primarily for visually handicapped children, the story of Little Shaggy and Little Rough, in raised textured shapes accompanied by printed text, enables both sighted and visually handicapped to share the book.

However, other handicapped children also benefit from tactile experiences and this particular book provides an additional aid to comprehension of the concepts and actualities of rough, smooth, circle and square.

Ordinary children and adults also gain experience of another dimension, learning through touch, and I have watched many a normal person seriously attempting to follow the story by means of his fingers, a salutory experience which usually leaves the sighted person aware of the untrained sensitivity of his finger tips.

2 Scratch and sniff, pop-up and 'squeaky' books provide an opportunity to use the senses and there are many such books on the market. In each case the life span is unlikely to be long and it may be necessary to restrict their use to times when an adult can control the handling. The fragrance fades after much scratching, the pictures fail to pop-up if manhandled and the squeak is silenced by excessive pressure. There are books accompanied by a mirror, for example Marion Walters' *This is Annette* (Deutsch, 1971) or devised to alter the picture by means of overlays, for example, Robin Ellis, (ed.) *The Double Colour 1, 2, 3 Book*, (Perceptua, 1973) and the children may need a helping hand with these.

3 The strength of rag or cloth books and of board (thick card pages) books is a useful asset. It is necessary to ensure that the rag books are non-toxic as they are likely to be chewed by some children. Rounded corners on the board books also help to ensure safety from otherwise potentially damaging, sharp-corner accidents. The Bodley Head board books are good examples as are the Chatto and Windus Flap Books. Concertina strips, using board, can also provide pleasure and information, for example, *Farmyard* by Brimax of Cambridge.

4 Single pictures, laminated, are commercially available or can be laminated by the library. They can offer specific information in an easily handled format, washable and with multi-purpose possibilities.

5 Kits and games, commonly found in public library children's departments are also useful in school libraries. There are chess, jigsaws and other board games with adapted versions for the blind of chess, beetle, card games and dominoes, and deaf sign language playing cards and adaptations for hand or arm disabled children. These are also part of the stock of toy libraries.

6 Charts and posters for communication and instruction and imaginative stimulation are available, many of them free. Publishers frequently provide, for sale or free, wall posters depicting series or themes from their books. Commercial

producers offer helpful step-by-step charts to show grooming, home activities, and activities in the community, which can provide the handicapped child with a visual approach to information and the learning of skills.

The criteria for selection of such materials include those of content, relevance, visual appeal and ease of handling. There is the need to provide, particularly for the mentally handicapped child, stimuli through sight, sound, smell and touch, all of which are available in book form. Some published lists of recommended books include:

Hearing impaired

Robertson, Mary Lett. Materials, programme suggestions for hearing impaired children. *School Media Quarterly*, vol. 4, no. 3, Spring 1976, pp. 263–68. Annotated, with age, ability and interest gradings.

Visually handicapped

Marshall, Margaret R. *Seeing Clear: books for the partially sighted child.* Oxford: School Library Association, 1977.

Simpson, Ray D. Books for children with limited vision. *Ontario Library Review*, vol. 55, no. 2, 1971, pp. 128–40.

Mentally handicapped

Marshall, Margaret R. *Each According to his Ability: a list of books and other visual material for use by and with mentally handicapped children.* Oxford: School Library Association, 1975.

Audio-visual material

Many commercial firms supply stories on disc, tape and cassette for example, Chivers of Bath, England; some with accompanying filmstrips, for example, Weston Woods (PO Box 2, Henley on Thames, Oxfordshire), who also provide movies, and Pinnacle Story Cassettes (available at many shops).

Information tapes and film material are also widely available in many countries, though some are not suitable for certain handicaps. The visually handicapped child probably makes most use of audio-visual media and equipment, and detail is given in the chapter on the visually handicapped child.

Catalogues of audio-visual materials are numerous, ranging from national, local, government and commercial catalogues to those of educational organizations and scientific and technical associations.

In addition, national libraries of one kind or another record books, for example, the National Listening Library in Britain and the Library of Congress Division for the Blind and Physically Handicapped in America. In addition to recording books at normal speed, the latter has, since 1967, produced recordings of books read at the rate of 125–150 words per minute rather than at the normal rate of 175–200 words per minute with ten second pauses between pages, so that the teacher or parent can repeat phrases or converse with the child about the page. A few bars of music at the start catches the child's attention. In some cases the recording loaned was accompanied by the print copy, but the cost became prohibitive and the print copy was discontinued. The slower speed enables the child of slow mind and the hearing impaired child to gain maximum benefit from the recording. Many other countries have a national listening library which supplies talking books to those registered as needing the service.

Many librarians and teachers record stories for in-school or in-library listening and these are very popular, as are the radio readings offered in some countries. In the USA there are about seventy stations, forty-one open channel, providing this entertainment, and in Britain too, both radio and TV have storytelling/reading programmes.

Visual series on television include the British Broadcasting Corporation's *Let's Go* series, the first produced for the mentally handicapped by any national broadcasting organization. Aimed at those with an IQ of 35 upwards, each programme lasts for twelve minutes and covers an activity familiar to many, such as *Let's Go Shopping*, *Let's Go to the Centre* (Training Centre), *Let's Go and Clean our Teeth*, *Let's Telephone*. A mentally handicapped person is shown succeeding in such an activity, and music, animation, carefully worded script and much recapitulation contribute towards the intended success of the mentally handicapped viewer in these activities. Also available are illustrated notes for teachers and parents and slide kits and storyboards of the programmes.

Television for the deaf in Britain includes a series called *Vision On*, a magazine programme for deaf children, and *In Sight*, a new (1980) series for use with hearing impaired pupils aged nine to thirteen. 'Stimulating visual material' is intended to develop language and reading skills and encourage confidence in writing and verbalizing'. (*Visual Education*, February 1979, p. 19.)

There is a large amount of film material, movies, filmstrips, slides and video recordings, which can be assessed against the criteria needed for the handicapped child.

Some English suppliers of tapes include:

British Library of Tape Recordings for Hospital Patients, Pullman House, 91 Goswell Road, London EC1V 7ER. Free lending but special playback machine with trolley, headsets and pillow phones.

Pinnacle Electronics Ltd, Electron House, Cray Avenue, St Mary Cray, Orpington, Kent BR5 3QJ. Pinnacle *Storytellers*, *Playtime* and *Musical Storytellers*.

National Listening Library, 49 Great Cumberland Place, London W1H 7LH. Special reproducer cassette player needed.

Weston Woods, PO Box 2, Henley on Thames, Oxfordshire.

Chivers Book Sales Ltd, 93–100 Locksbrook Road, Bath, Avon.

The features required for selection for the handicapped child include those required for print material in terms of content and structure and illustrative information. In addition, in the case of story or information material, there are basic features to look for:

1 Audio

Quality of sound – particularly for the hearing impaired. Length – related to concentration span.

Suitability for age/ability – thematic or conceptual difficulty.

Speed of reading – in relation to:

(a) assimilation mentally.
(b) hearing ability.
(c) following the tape in a printed text.

Relationship to visual, in matching of word content to picture content (soundtrack to film material), any discrepancy between the two causing confusion to mentally or hearing impaired children, i.e. the words must not say more than can be seen. If the audio material is for visually handicapped listeners, the information content needs to take account of the lack of visual knowledge by using adequate verbal description.

Compatibility of voice to picture, so as not to detract from one or the other. The 'right' voice adds comprehension, atmosphere and possibly additional tonal information.

2 Visual
Clarity of photographic content, whether black and white or colour, in terms of clearly depicting the aspect in such a way as to achieve the specific objective of that clip, slide, photograph. Clarity of visible text, whether on overhead projector, transparency, video, in balloon talk, print or strip or other design for putting text on the screen. Computer produced teletext is still to improve in this respect.

3 Technical
Ease of use of the medium by/with children

- supervised or unsupervised, the potential teaching/learning use.
- classroom, library, home, individual, group, informative, motivative and creative use.
- availability of appropriate equipment.
- availability of appropriate viewing/listening facilities.

Named examples are not given here, as there are many sources of information on specific audio-visual materials, ranging from the bibliographies and catalogues of national organizations, to the libraries for the blind, the physically handicapped and the visually handicapped, talking book centres and commercial organizations supplying a variety of material and equipment, to the recommendations given by individual subject teachers and librarians.

Material about handicapped children
Selection of material *about* handicapped children is useful but, unless being used for bibliotherapy, should be selected in no greater quantity than for the ordinary child.

The blind, deaf or physically handicapped child is not necessarily restricted in his imagination or his ability to enjoy books about children looking, listening and actively moving about in exciting adventures. Though these may be 'foreign' to the handicapped child, the situation is no different from an English or American child reading a story set in another country or another historical period. Most children in small language countries, for example, Norway and Holland, have had little choice but to read translations of books from other countries.

It is thus wrong to suppose that handicapped children want to read about handicapped children, except in the normal course of reading like ordinary children.

However, it *is* important for ordinary children to read such books in order to create a greater awareness of both the normality of the handicapped child and his differences. The difficulty here lies in selecting those books which do not deride, belittle or magnify the handicap out of context, which do not present a false, sentimental, 'sympathetic' picture of the child.

There are, in many countries, lists of books about the handicapped child. I include here several examples.

1 From Northern Ireland, *Reach Out: a list of fiction and biography about handicapped children and teenagers*, 1979, produced by Belfast Public Libraries as part of the programme for the International Year of the Child. About fifty titles are annotated.

2 *The Other Child: a Bodley Head Booklist*, 1979, a simple list of books covered by this title, published by Bodley Head.

3 The International Youth Library, Munich. *Das Geistig und Körperlich Behinderte Kind im Kinder- und Jugendbuch.* Duplicated list of books about the handicapped child.

4 Bradford Public Libraries, England. School Services Centre. *Stories about the handicapped.* Duplicated list.

5 Barbara Baskind and K. Harris. *Notes from a Different Drummer: a guide to juvenile fiction portraying the handicapped.* New York: Bowker, 1978.

They include a variety of books such as those about deaf children, for example, Freddy Bloom's little picture book *The Boy who Couldn't Hear*, London: Bodley Head, 1977, and Elizabeth Browning's *I Can't See What You're Saying*, Elek, 1977; those about physically handicapped children, for example, Susan Burke's *Alexander in Trouble*, London: Bodley Head, 1979, about a boy in a wheelchair, and June Epstein's *Boy on Sticks*, Abbotsford, Australia: National Press, 1979, about a boy with spina bifida; those about visual handicap, for example, Jean

Little's *From Anna*, New York: Harper and Row, 1972, and Helen Keller's *Story of My Life*, Westhaven: Pendulum Press, 1974; those about mental handicaps, for example, Hanne Larsen's *Don't Forget Tom*, London: A & C Black, 1975, and Patricia Wrightson's *I Own the Racecourse*, London: Hutchinson, 1968 and Colby F. Rodowsky's *What About Me?* London: Watts, 1976; and those about speech impediments, for example, Kim Platt's *The Boy Who Could Make Himself Disappear*, New York: Dell, 1971.

The Scandinavian countries led the way in publishing picture books about handicapped children and other countries have since increased the number of picture books, strips and biographical works about handicapped people. These, if written without sentimentality, serve to transmit to the non-handicapped, some understanding of the difficulties experienced by the handicapped, and serve to emphasize the normality of most handicapped people.

The selector of books for the handicapped child has the same objectives as the person selecting books for the ordinary child, the creation of a library stock which will:

(a) stimulate language.
(b) provide identification.
(c) develop understanding.
(d) add colour.
(e) reinforce existing language.
(f) add to existing language.
(g) create a shared experience between the mind of the child and the mind of the writer or illustrator.

But he also has the task of looking for materials which pay particular attention to the features which provide extra help for the child whose handicap forms a barrier to the achievement of these objectives. A library's effectiveness is based upon the adequacy of its stock to serve the needs of its users.

Chapter Twelve

Design and equipment

NOT ALL HANDICAPPED PEOPLE have the same problems of access to and use of a library, and librarians serving a specific handicap attempt to provide accommodation to fit the specific need.

In general terms, problems arise when the handicapped person wants to use a public facility such as the public library or the library in an ordinary school or college. Although there are recommendations and requirements laid down in some countries regarding such buildings they tend to apply to new rather than existing buildings. The Unesco Manifesto says: 'The public library should be centrally situated, accessible to the physically handicapped and open at times convenient to the user.'[1]

In Britain, the 1970 Chronically Sick and Disabled Persons Act, and in the USA, the Title lv(b) of the Library Services and Construction Act 1966, stipulate the ways in which access must be facilitated to public buildings. The design requirements are indicated in the American *Standards Specifications for Making Buildings and Facilities Accessible To, and Usable By, the Physically Handicapped*, 1970, and the British Standards Institute, *Access for the Disabled to Buildings*, 1967.

But adaptations to existing buildings, and thought and action on the interior layout are necessary, particularly in the intended, or newly integrated schools.

Information on detailed design, planning and safety features is available in much of the professional literature, the intention in this section being to indicate those aspects which hitherto may not have impinged upon the average librarian's awareness.

As suggested in the chapter on public library service, the handicapped child may arrive at the library by car and it is necessary for car parks to provide bays for the disabled, signposted by a symbol or other label to indicate that the space is reserved for a disabled driver or vehicle carrying a disabled passenger, the siting of those spaces to be as near as possible to easy access to the building.

Ramps are needed for those unable to manage steps, but there are physically handicapped people who cannot cope with ramps, so both are required. Ramps need a minimum width of four feet and a gradient which can be coped with, unaided, by someone in a wheelchair. Both ramps and steps need a handrail, so that the visually and physically handicapped can be guided or supported. Automatic doors are a help to the majority of handicapped people.

In general, all libraries must amend regulations about wheeled vehicles and dogs in order to give access to wheelchairs and guide dogs. In general there should be unisex lavatories so that the handicapped who need to be accompanied, are not prevented from using the facilities because the accompanying person is of the opposite sex.

Flooring should be non-slip, and normally a carpet is advocated because it reduces sound distraction for the deaf and visually handicapped, but it should be a tight-weave rather than deep-pile carpet, to aid walking handicapped people and wheelchair users.

Lighting in libraries is normally given special attention, but extra care needs to be taken to provide non-glare surfaces whether floor, shelf or table surfaces, and individually controlled angle lights in reading spaces, so that visually handicapped readers have the minimum of light distraction.

Care must be taken to avoid protruding angles, furniture, signs, and other potential hazards for the partially sighted and the physically handicapped.

It may be necessary to have extra electrical outlets for the special equipment and reading aids needed for effective use of the library by some handicapped people, and for communication between staff and users. Communication boards for the deaf and speech impaired are also useful pieces of equipment. Suitable listening/viewing facilities for audio-visual use are also needed.

Certain handicaps require particular attention to design, layout and equipment. The physically handicapped child, if in a wheelchair, will need a ramp to get into the building; wide corridors, doorways and toilet cubicles; adequate space in elevators; an absence of steps and door sills and apronless tables without protruding legs, at a height of about twenty-nine inches.

Ambulant physically handicapped children may need a range of seating, such as high level chairs, beanbags and floor cushions; card catalogues, side by side rather than one on top of another and clear pathways round the library and shelving, both static and wheeled, which do not involve stooping or reaching high.

All need automatic doors or failing those, lightweight doors with lever handles, rather than swing doors, and with kick plates and see-through panels.

The visually handicapped child benefits from a library with good lighting and textured walking surfaces where floor furniture is well spaced and in identifiable layout.

Per-Gunnar Braf's book on *The Physical Environment and the Visually Handicapped*[2] is a mine of information on the extraordinary number of hazards in the average street and building of which the sighted person is normally unaware, but which can cause difficulties and damage to the visually handicapped person.

Notices and instructions normally put on library walls need to be in large print and braille or in tactile symbols. Tape recorded guides to the library, accessions lists, notices and other library information put on tape are helpful to the child unable to read print or braille.

The hearing impaired person may need little extra building design and layout attention, other than to the acoustics which can powerfully aid or powerfully confuse; a loop system into which the hearing handicapped can plug their aids; and the electrical outlets needed for the teletext and other equipment mentioned later in this chapter.

Examples of libraries which have attempted to provide accommodation suitable for special needs include:

1 The Alabama Regional Library for the Blind and Physically Handicapped, which is barrier free, has handrails to guide users to automatic sliding doors, raised tactile maps of the interior, a teletypewriter service, and makes use of sign language.

2 At the Henshaw School for the Visually Handicapped in

Harrogate, England, the library, like the rest of the school, has colourful decor and wall pictures, part of a positive policy to provide colour for those with some sight, and interest and colour information for those with none. The shelving is well spaced, with maximum height at four feet six inches, and there are large table surfaces to facilitate the use of large print and braille volumes and to allow for the extra 'personal' space needed.

3 Gallaudet College, Washington, the Model School for the Deaf (MSSD), founded in 1970, was designed with emphasis on the visual and the tactile, with colour and comfort. There are conversation pits throughout the school where the young people are encouraged to 'talk' to each other, and outside there are areas so designed that the students can communicate in sign language without being seen by others, an important feature in a school where the signing person who can be seen by others, can also be 'read' by others. The use of video equipment and other audio-visual media in the classroom is strongly reflected in the library also.

All these aspects were mentioned in the answers to a questionnaire sent to societies concerned with handicapped children in Yorkshire (Appendix 5), asking what provision they thought public libraries should make for handicapped children. Summarized, the suggestions were:

(a) physical provision: parking space, ramps, rails, elevators, non-slip floors, wide doorways, good lighting, interior circulation space, and adapted toilets.
(b) equipment provision: talking book machines, cassette recorders, loop systems, reading aids, wheelchairs, appropriate table heights, magnifying aids, large-print typewriters, and headsets.

The returned questionnaire which had been sent to all the public library authorities in Yorkshire, asking what each provided in these two respects, revealed that few could match the societies' expectations.

Where handicapped children and young people can use a library, in terms of ability and interest or school need, it is necessary to ensure that they are not further disabled by the library's barriers to use, which are often erected unwittingly. As more children are integrated into ordinary schools and colleges it is perhaps timely for librarians to look again at their libraries and to check on ease of access to and availability of equipment.

Reading aids

The handicapped child who needs reading aids when not in the library needs them also when he *is* in the library, though he may not always find them there.

Some children will bring to the library their own portable reading aids, such as magnifiers and amplifiers, but many can be helped to more comfortable and more efficient reading and communication by means of some of the items described here.

The intention is not to provide a comprehensive list of aids and their suppliers, but to give an indication of the range of available aids, with just a few examples of specific named items. Detailed information on particular makes of equipment can be obtained from several sources, for instance the Library of Congress Division for the Blind and Physically Handicapped in Washington, and the Royal National Institute for the Blind, and the Disabled Living Foundation, in London.

Some of the aids described are useful for the actual process of reading, some for the kind of work done with books by users of libraries, such as making notes, and some for communication between child and librarian or child and teacher, in the library. Even if librarians cannot supply all these items for reasons of finance, it is necessary for them to know of the existence of such forms of aid to reading and library use.

1 Typewriters. The range of typewriters available for handicapped people includes the following:
   - (a) Ordinary typewriters, for which numerous attachments are available to enable the motor impaired person to use the machine effectively.
   - (b) Silent typewriters for use in public places like libraries.
   - (c) Large-print typewriters for the visually handicapped.
   - (d) POSSUM (Patient Operated Selector Mechanism, enabling a person to operate the typewriter by means of toes, mouth or other parts of the body.

(e) Talking typewriters, which store typed information and speak it back with synthetic voice via magnetic tape or computer.
(f) Remote controlled typing systems, operated by keyboards of varying sizes and shapes to cater for varying handicaps.
(g) Communicators. These are mini electronic typewriters, an example of which is the Canon Communicator, a battery-powered electronic typewriter which straps onto the wrist, leg or chair arm. About the size of a pocket calculator, it can be operated by tapping the keys with the fingers or, for those with finger difficulty, a pencil or mouth or foot operated object. Messages are printed on tape at ten characters per second, and emerge clearly visible.

2 Microprocessors, word processors. These consist of an alphabetic keyboard containing basic words. When the keys are pressed the words are transmitted to the television screen or visual display unit. In the more sophisticated word processors, words and lines can be juxtaposed, rearranged, altered or deleted at the press of a key. These are commercially available and in use in many large organizations to speed up secretarial and clerical work. The potential for use by handicapped people and libraries is enormous.

3 Teleprinters. These machines and their adaptations are in common use, for example the Phonetype, which is an acoustic coupling device linking a teleprinter to the telephone. When the telephone rings a light flashes to warn the hearing handicapped person and the message appears in type on the teleprinter. This enables the deaf to use a telephone if there is a link-up service.

4 Visual systems. This term covers a variety of aids, including:
(a) the overhead projector, which is in common use.
(b) the closed-circuit television system, capable of magnifying print up to forty-five times, which enables people with low residual vision to read the printed word.
(c) CEEFAX, a data broadcasting system offered by the

BBC, which provides teletext screen-sized pages of news and other information, transmitted by means of a control unit and selector keypad which can be connected to the normal television set. Used mainly for relaying a variety of information of general interest, it also provides subtitles for some recorded programmes, thus enabling the deaf person to enjoy at least some of the normal television programmes.

(d) PRESTEL, a similar information service offered by the Post Office, though not specifically for handicapped people. It provides information on the subscriber's television screen which is linked to the subscriber's telephone; this, in turn, is linked to the data base on the Post Office's computer system. Its use in big commercial organizations is increasing and many large libraries with an important information function are also subscribers.

5 Print reading systems. These hold out a great hope for those who cannot read print by the usual means. Examples include Opticon, which is a basic kit comprising of hand-held scanner which is passed over the printed page, producing signals which are translated on to a tactile pad and then detected or 'read' by the index finger. Attachments include typewriter, calculator, visual display unit and small-print magnifiers.

Thus a blind or partially sighted person may read print which has been converted into a series of vibrating tactual patterns.

The Kurzweil Autoscan reading machine also translates the printed word but directly into synthetic speech. It reads and prints materials at 250 words a minute.

6 Braille systems. In addition to the traditional Perkins brailler used by the majority of braillists, there are electronic machines such as the VersaBraille system, which records braille and audio information on cassette tape and reproduces it on a twenty character line of braille cells. Revisions and deletions can be made without re-brailling any other part of the page and each C-60 cassette can hold four hundred pages of braille.

Braille print-out machines can now be linked to a computer for speedier, accurate and less costly transcription.

7 Speech aids. Machines which speak back the printed word can aid the child with a speech or hearing disability, or the child who has vision problems. Talking typewriters; speech plus calculators, which speak back the normal arithmetical calculations; and communication units such as the Bliss Communication Unit and Kurzweil Autoscan.

8 Recording and playback items. Examples include special talking book reproducers, the use of which is required by both the British National Listening Library and by the American Library of Congress Division for the Blind and Physically Handicapped in their loan of recordings. These, plus special switches, amplifiers and headphones, are available as needed by registered 'readers'.

The British Library of Tape Recordings for Hospital Patients has a free tape service and a special playback machine with trolley, headsets and pillow phones for easier use in hospital.

9 Page turners. For those who are unable to hold a book or turn pages there are aids which can be operated by mouth, foot, headband, magnet, electricity or battery.

Electronic turners include, for example, the American Saltus Reader, a portable box that holds books, magazines or specially printed scrolls of popular books, which can be advanced or rewound by means of a switch.

10 Bookrests. These may be needed by those who must have reading materials at a particular angle for maximum vision, and by those unable to hold a book. There is a British Standards specification for such items, BS 5043;1973.

Rests include adjustable angled lecterns for floor or table; perspex tilted frames for clamping to bed or wheelchair, or free standing; tilted tables and cantilever desks which are commonly found in special schools and libraries, providing a reading and writing surface with wheelchair clearance; and shaped foam cushions placed in the lap, on which the book may be rested.

There are many other items of equipment and attachments, such as amplifiers and magnifying aids, which are supplied by schools, hospitals, communication systems, commercial firms and libraries, though few countries specify what should be available in public libraries. *The American Standards for Library Services for the Blind and Visually Handicapped* say that large public libraries should make accessible:

1 At least one standard typewriter for use by readers.
2 Suitable optical aids in adequate quantity.
3 At least one large print typewriter, and additional ones as needed.
4 At least one braille recorder, and additional ones as needed.
5 At least one tape recorder, and additional ones as needed.
6 At least one 4 speed record player or talking book machine, and additional ones as needed.
7 Oversize tables, shelves, catalogue trays etc. as required by the special nature of the materials to be handled.[3]

The inclusion of this information here, is intended to emphasize the fact that visually and other handicapped children who have been used to these aids in their special schools, will be handicapped without them when visiting their public library, and later, when they have left school and its facilities, will be plunged into an adult life where a public, academic or other institutional library without these aids, is, in effect, closed to them.

Many of the aids described are expensive for an individual but could be purchased for library use. Of particular importance if priorities are sought, are those aids which can translate the printed word into a form accessible to those who cannot read print. This opens up the whole world of books previously available only to the ordinary reader, a world often longed for by the special reader.

Chapter Thirteen

Conclusion

The Warnock Committee asked those submitting evidence to state in one sentence their main message to the Committee. The Invalid Children's Aid Association (ICAA), in its submitted evidence, emphasized that all concerned with special education should ensure that the child with a handicap does not emerge from school as a handicapped person. The librarian's part in achieving this aim can be summarized in Twelve Commandments. Thou shalt:

1 Train thyself to understand and serve the needs of the handicapped child.
2 Select appropriate material, as indicated throughout the book.
3 Facilitate class visits to the library.
4 Make professional visits to special schools and hospitals for the handicapped child.
5 Co-ordinate volunteers for story sessions.
6 Encourage mobile children to join normal activities.
7 Ask planners to provide ramps, lifts, wide-opening doors, non-slip floors etc, as indicated in the planning and design section.
8 Persuade publishers to produce books with:
   (a) black type on white paper.
   (b) adaptations for special users.
   (c) stronger paper and binding.
   (d) suitable content in theme, vocabulary and illustration.
9 Liaise with teachers for visits, project work, loans, and talks on books and libraries to associations of teachers, parents' groups and education authority courses.
10 Liaise with health services: doctors, nurses, health visitors,

psychologists, psychiatrists, hospital librarians and social workers.

11 Liaise with parents to provide an information service on aspects like social services; local societies for the handicapped; special journals and books on the handicap; books for their children; and talks to local associations for handicaps.

12 Train thy library staff to understand the needs, the problems and the joys of the handicapped child and his family.

There is no reason why most children with handicaps, whether physical, mental, aural, visual or emotional, should not enjoy books, whether they can read or not, *and* benefit from them, for books are in themselves therapeutic exercises. One of the main aims of therapy is to encourage and develop the following:

1 Physical dexterity, which is needed to pick up a book, to turn the pages, whether rag, board or paper, a task which able bodied adults find difficult, hence the licking of the finger to aid the turning of a page; and digital dexterity, which is needed to point at and touch objects in the pictures or to touch the thermoplastic or tactual surfaces of many books.

2 Eye movements. The need to learn to move the eyes from left to right when reading, and the effort to focus on pictures or colour definition.

3 Speech, which can be encouraged by books without words, picture stimulation and reading of words, including conversation arising from the words or pictures.

4 Hearing and listening, which are developed through being read to or in storytelling, or by the child reading aloud.

5 Mental exercise, resulting in comprehension for the able child and recognition for the least able child.

6 The ability to derive educational benefits, not necessarily in the school sense, but in the enjoyment of learning informally in leisure time or play, from books and related materials.

7 The ability to derive emotional benefits, as the child is

transported to the world of the imagination; trying on another identity through story characters and situations.

8 A sense of smell, both from the normal smell of paper and print and from scratch and sniff books.

9 A sense of taste. The use of all the senses is common in most children and many handicapped children do lick or chew books and may do so in safety with most non-toxic rag books.

10 The ability to enjoy.

All of these faculties can be developed by the use of one piece of equipment – the book – with the result that the handicapped child is able to derive increased enjoyment from the use of books, which provides the greatest motivation for further reading.

References

Chapter 1

1 E. Younghusband, *et. al. Living with Handicap.* London: National Children's Bureau, 1970, p. 2.
2 Jessie Parfit. *Emotional Disturbance in Handicapped Children.* Highlight, no. 9. London: National Children's Bureau, 1974, p. 4.
3 Department of Education and Science. *Education Statistics for the United Kingdom, 1975.* London: HMSO, 1978.
4 E. Marais. Opening doors only to close them? *Times Educational Supplement,* 21 September 1978, p. 47.

Chapter 2

1 Mary Warnock. *Special Educational Needs: report of the Committee of Enquiry into the education of handicapped children and young people.* London: HMSO, 1978.
2 Warnock, *op. cit.*, p. 270.
3 Warnock, *op. cit.*, p. 96.
4 Malcolm Parlett. *Towards Integration: a study of blind and partially sighted children in ordinary schools.* London: National Foundation for Educational Research, 1976.
5 Jessie Parfit and M. Jobling. *IRMMH Research Centre on Handicap in Children: final report on the experimental project.* London: Institute for Research into Mental and Multiple Handicap, 1977.
6 Parfit, *op. cit.*, p. 12.
7 Jean Carnett. Towards integration: special children in a comprehensive school. *Rathbone News,* June 1977, pp. 45–9.
8 B. S. Bloom. Mastery of learning and its implication for curriculum development. *In* M. Golby (ed.) *Curriculum Development.* London: Croom Helm, 1975, pp. 334–50; p. 339.
9 Simon H. Haskell, Elizabeth K. Barrett and Helen Taylor. *The Education of the Motor and Neurologically Handicapped Child.* London: Croom Helm, 1977, p. 56.
10 Haskell, *op. cit.*, p. 56.
11 Sarane S. Boocock. *An Introduction to the Sociology of Learning.* Boston: Houghton Mifflin, 1972.
12 Samuel A. Kirk and G. Orville Johnson. *Educating the Retarded Child.* Boston: Houghton Mifflin, 1951, p. 270.
13 Kirk and Johnson, *op. cit.*, pp. 259–60.

14 American Library Association. *Standards for Library Services for the Blind and Visually Handicapped.* Chicago: ALA, 1967.
15 Elizabeth Johnson and Thelma Merriweather. Blind children learn to relate. *American Libraries,* vol. 1, February 1970, pp. 168–9.
16 Ruth M. White. Light in a dark world. *In* Maryalls G. Strom (ed.) *Library Service to the Blind and Physically Handicapped.* New Jersey: Scarecrow, 1977, pp. 124–33.
17 Bob Jerrolds. Preparing librarians to help the disabled reader. *Wilson Library Bulletin,* May 1976, p. 719.
18 Ken Morgan. The school library and children with learning and behaviour problems. *In* B. H. Baskin and K. Harris (eds.) *The Special Child in the Library.* Chicago: ALA, 1976, pp. 117–19.
19 Eliza T. Dresang. There are no other children. *School Library Journal,* September 1977, pp. 19–23.

Chapter 3

1 The British Mental Health Act, 1959. London: HMSO, 1959.
2 British Psychological Society. *Children in Hospitals for the Subnormal: report.* London: British Psychological Society, 1966.
3 Russell Miller. Unlocking the doors. *Sunday Times Colour Supplement,* 13 March 1977, pp. 32–42.
4 Charles H. Hallas. *The Care and Training of the Mentally Subnormal.* Bristol: Wright, 1978, p. 11.
5 Leonora Secker. Sex education and mental handicap. *Special Education,* vol. 62, no. 1, March 1973, pp. 27–8.
6 Dorothy Butler. *Cushla and Her Books.* London: Hodder and Stoughton, 1979.
7 Margaret Polack. Bringing up Ruth. *Parents Voice,* vol. 25, no. 1, March 1975, pp. 24–5.
8 Margaret R. Marshall. *Each According to his Ability: a list of books and other visual material for use by and with mentally handicapped children.* Oxford: School Library Association, 1975.
9 Tordis Ørjasæter. *Boka on Dag Tore.* Oslo: Cappelens, 1976.
10 Butler, *op. cit.*, p. 93.

Chapter 4

1 Mary Brennan. *Can Deaf Children Acquire Language? An evaluation of linguistic principles in deaf education.* London: British Deaf Association, 1976.
2 C. K. Bliss and S. McNaughton. The book to the film *Mr Symbol Man.* Canada: The National Film Board of Canada and Australia, 1974, and, S. McNaughton, *et al. Teaching Guidelines.* Toronto: Blissymbolic Communication Foundation, 1975.

3 McCoy Vernon. *Total Communication: the human right of deaf children and their families*. London: British Deaf Association, 1974, p. 2.
4 David M. Denton. *The Philosophy of Total Communication*. London: British Deaf Association, 1976, p. 4.
5 Freddy Bloom. *The Boy who Couldn't Hear*. London: Bodley Head, 1977.
6 Edward C. Merrill. *The Responsibility of the Professionals to the Deaf Consumer*. London: British Deaf Association, 1976, p. 1.
7 National College of Teachers of the Deaf and Society of Teachers of the Deaf. *The Hearing Impaired Child in Your Class*. London: NCTD and STD, 1976.
8 Boyce Rensberger. For the deaf the language gap is unbridgeable. *New York Times*, 22 April 1979, p. 29.
9 Eugene D. Mindel and McCoy Vernon. *They Grow in Silence: the deaf child and his family*. Maryland: National Association of the Deaf, 1976, Table 2, p. 91.
10 D. C. Wollman and Joan Hickmott. Language development for deaf pupils. *Dialogue*, Schools Council Newsletter, no. 23, 1976, pp. 6–7.
11 Gisela Freytag. Bibliotherapy by means of picture books for speech handicapped children. *International Library Review*, vol. 9, no. 2, 1977, pp. 197–203.
12 Patricia Blair Corey. *School Library Services for Deaf Children*. Washington D.C.: Alexander Graham Bell Association, 1960.
13 Jean and Gareth Adamson. *Topsy and Tim at School*. London: Blackie and Home Library for the Deaf, 1968.
14 Joanne C. Jensen. The library and the deaf child. *Catholic Library World*, vol. 45, no. 9, April 1974, pp. 426–28.
15 Virginia Guldager. Communication and the multiply handicapped child. Perkins School for the Blind, Watertown, Massachusetts (mimeo).

Chapter 5

1 International Year of the Child Secretariat. *Should Prevention of Blindness be Your Emphasis for IYC?* IYC report no. 9. New York: IYC, April 1978, p. 4.
2 Remy Charlip and Mary Beth. *Handtalk: an ABC of fingerspelling and sign language*. New York: Parents, 1974.
3 Vasile Adamescu. How do I perceive the world? *Braille Review*, no. 4, 1973. Viata Nova appendix.
4 Virginia Allan Jensen and Dorcas Woodbury Haller. *What's That?* Denmark: Forlaget IBIS, 1977 and London: Collins, 1979.
5 Library Association and National Association for the Education

of the Partially Sighted. *Print for the Visually Handicapped Reader: papers and proceedings of a conference, 1970*. LA publication no. 6, London: LA, 1971, p. 57, and Alison Shaw, *Print for Partial Sight: a report to the Library Association Sub-Committee on books for readers with defective sight*. London: LA, 1969.

Chapter 6

1 Sally Gray *et. al.* Sally and company are leaving. *Link*, (the journal of the Association for Spina Bifida and Hydrocephalus) September/October 1975, pp. 8–9.
2 Association for Spina Bifida and Hydrocephalus. *Children with Spina Bifida in School: a booklet for teachers and students*. London: ASBH, 1978.
3 Ruth A. Vellerman. The school library in the education of handicapped children. *Rehabilitation Literature*, vol. 32, no. 5, May 1971, pp. 138–40.

Chapter 7

1 R. Pill and R. Jacobs. Report on a pilot study on the problems of long-stay children in hospitals. Swansea: University of Swansea, 1974 (mimeo).
2 National Union of Teachers. *Teaching in Hospital Schools*. London: NUT, 1973, p. 4.
3 National Association of Hospital Teachers. *Hospital Schools in England and Wales*. London: NAHT, 1976, p. 3.
4 National Association of Hospital Teachers, *op. cit.*, p. 3.
5 Eileen E. Cumming. Children in hospital: do they need a library service? *Book Trolley*, vol. 3, no. 3, September 1971, pp. 3–9.
6 Library Association, Hospital Libraries Group. Sick and handicapped children: report of a joint meeting with the Youth Libraries Group held at Great Ormond Street Hospital, 1973. *Health and Welfare Libraries Quarterly*, vol. 1, no. 1, March 1974, pp. 12–13.
7 Eleanor Phinney. *The Library and the Patient: an introduction to library services for patients in health care institutions*. Chicago: ALA, 1977, pp. 54–9.
8 National Union of Teachers, *op. cit.*, p. 4.
9 Mary B. Davison. Libraries in hospital schools. *National Froebel Foundation Bulletin*, June 1961, pp. 10–12.
10 Gerald Bramley. *Outreach: library services for the institutionalized, the elderly and the physically handicapped*. London: Bingley, 1978, p. 43.

Chapter 8

1 Bjørg Heie. Literature and library services for the handicapped in Norway. *Scandinavian Public Libraries Quarterly*, vol. 9, nos. 3/4, 1976, pp. 192–7.
2 Moraye I. Atinma. Public and school library services to the physically handicapped in Nigeria: an evaluation. *International Library Review*, vol. 1, no. 4, October 1979, pp. 441–9; p. 449.
3 Philadelphia Public Library. *ALA Bulletin*, vol. 55, no. 4, April 1961, p. 320.
4 Fay Winkworth and Helen Sunderland. *Public Library Facilities for Handicapped Children in Yorkshire: survey and directory*. Leeds: Library Association. Youth Libraries Group, Yorkshire Branch, 1976.
5 R. N. Lock (ed.) *Manual of Library Economy*. London: Bingley, 1977, chapter 12, pp. 260–75.
6 Janet Hill. Playgroup for mentally handicapped children. *Hertfordshire County Libraries Newsletter*, 1976.

Chapter 9

1 Charles Smith. A toy library for handicapped children. *Australian Library Journal*, vol. 25, no. 4, May 1976, pp. 142–44.
2 Annie C. Dwyer *et. al. South Australian Toy Libraries: a survey. 1976.* Adelaide: South Australia Institute of Technology, 1976.

Chapter 10

1 Elfrida Vipont and Raymond Briggs. *The Elephant and the Bad Baby*. London: Hamish Hamilton, 1968.

Chapter 11

1 Library Association. *Library Resource Provision in Schools: recommended guidelines.* London: LA, 1978.
2 American Library Association. *Standards for Library Services for the Blind and Visually Handicapped, op. cit.*

Chapter 12

1 *Unesco Bulletin for Libraries.* vol. 26, no. 3, May/June 1972, pp. 129–31.
2 Per-Gunnar Braf. *The Physical Environment and the Visually Handicapped.* Sweden: ICTA Information Centre, 1974.
3 American Library Association. *Standards for Library Services for the Blind and Visually Handicapped, op. cit.*, p. 45.

Appendix 1

Joint Meeting — IFLA Discussion Document

Questions to answer about your country.

1 Is there an organization in your country specifically concerned with mentally handicapped children?

2 Is the National Library responsible for
   (a) acquiring
   (b) storing
   (c) lending
   (d) promoting library service to mentally handicapped children?

3 Is there any library service to such children in special schools and hospitals?

4 Are there (a) bibliographies of books for mentally handicapped children.
   (b) library guidelines for service.

5 What do you think is the greatest need in your country?
   (a) more special schools and hospital schools.
   (b) more specially written/adapted books.
   (c) more understanding by librarians of such children's needs.
   (d) more provision of suitable material by libraries.
   (e) greater co-operation between organizations, libraries, schools and parents of such children.
   (f) co-operative networks.

6 What is your Library Association's role in this?

7 What is IFLA's Hospital and Children's Libraries Section's role in the provision of books for mentally handicapped children?

Please come prepared with information related to your country, bringing with you relevant documents if possible.

Jean Clarke. Chairman of the Hospital Libraries Section.

Margaret Marshall. Chairman of the Children's Libraries Section.

Appendix 2

Bibliotherapy: a select list of readings

BROWN, Eleanor F. Bibliotherapy and Its Widening Applications. New Jersey: Scarecrow, 1975.

HYNES, Arleen M. The Goals of Bibliotherapy. *Art Psychotherapy*, vol. 7, no. 1, pp. 001–007

KINNEY, Margaret. Bibliotherapy program: the requirements for training. *Library Trends*, vol. XL, no. 2, October 1962, pp. 127–35.

LEEDY, J. J. (ed.) *Poetry Therapy*. Philadephia: J. B. Lippincott, 1969.

LEEDY, J. J. (ed.) *Poetry the Healer*. Philadelphia: J. B. Lippincott, 1973.

LERNER, Arthur (ed.) *Poetry in the Therapeutic Experience*. New York: Pergamon Press, 1978.

LYONS, Grace. A Guide to the Bibliotherapy of the Mentally and Physically Handicapped. *Information Reports and Bibliographies*, vol. 7, no. 2.

MYERS, J. C. Library work with brain damaged patients: a new mode of bibliotherapy. *Bulletin of the Medical Library Association*, vol. 60, no. 2, April 1972, pp. 333–39.

RUBIN, Rhea Joyce (ed.) *Bibliotherapy Sourcebook*. London: Mansell, 1978.

RUBIN, Rhea Joyce (ed.) *Using Bibliotherapy: a guide to theory and techniques*. London: Mansell, 1978.

RUSSELL, Alma E. and Russell, William A. Using bibliotherapy with emotionally disturbed children. *Teaching Exceptional Children*, Summer 1979.

The American Library Association's Association of Specialized and Co-operative Library Agencies, Bibliotherapy Committee is at present preparing a book on current bibliotherapy projects in the library world.

Appendix 3

Home Library
Simple-Language Editions of Books for Children
A BREAKTHROUGH TRUST PROJECT

People concerned with children who experience problems in learning to read will be aware of the difficulty in finding attractive and suitable books for them. There is a need for books of the correct age interest that also present reading matter that is sufficiently simple. This problem is particularly evident with children whose progress in reading is affected by a disability.

Three years ago the Home Library, a voluntary scheme with the aim of providing deaf children with suitable books, was initiated. The method used is to paste labels printed with an easier version of the stories over the text in contemporary picture books for children.

People professionally involved with children, including children's librarians and teachers, have recognized the value of these books for use with other minority groups, as well as deaf children, creating a market that cannot reasonably be met by the present voluntary project.

This response has encouraged the organizers of the Home Library to approach publishers with the idea of printing simple-language editions of their own books for children, in the same way that foreign language editions are sometimes produced. It appears that this would be a feasible proposition, provided that concrete evidence of a market for simple-language editions can be shown.

An appeal is therefore being made to everyone who would welcome simple-language versions of popular books for children at the same prices as the originals. We would be grateful if you would complete the questionnaire below.

Further information about the Home Library can be obtained from:

JOHN WHEELER,
23 CANNING STREET, BRIGHTON, BN2 2EF.

A stamped, addressed envelope would be appreciated with enquiries.

Appendix 3

HOME LIBRARY QUESTIONNAIRE

(1) Do you feel that sufficient books are available for language deprived children?

YES. . . . NO. . . .

Fiction YES. . . . NO. . . . *Non-Fiction* YES. . . . NO. . . .

(2) Would you be interested in purchasing simple-language editions of contemporary picture books for children, at normal prices?

YES. . . . NO. . . .

(3) Can you estimate the number of copies you might purchase?

1 copy. . . . 5–10 copies. . . . 20–30 copies. . . .

2–5 copies. . . . 10–20 copies. . . . Over 30 copies. . . .

(4) In your opinion, which children would benefit from these books?

Deaf. . . . Partially Sighted. . . . Slow Learners. . . .

Ethnic Minority Groups. . . . Mentally Handicapped. . . .

Normal Children. . . . Others. . . .

(5) Have you any other comments or suggestions?

Name. . . . . *Position*. . . . .

Organization (if any). . . . .

Address . . . .

Please return to: JOHN WHEELER,
23 CANNING STREET, BRIGHTON, BN2 2EF.

Thank you.

RESULTS OF MARKET RESEARCH PROJECT

(1) Total number of questionnaires returned and analysed	. . . .	390
(2) Number not valid for purchase estimates	. . . .	18
(3) Purchase estimates:		
Minimum	. . . .	3,388
Maximum	. . . .	8,710
Average	. . . .	6,049

These figures are calculated from the following data given on returned questionnaires:

Prepared to buy 1 copy	. . . .	45
2–5 copies	. . . .	79
5–10 copies	. . . .	67
10–20 copies	. . . .	39
20–30 copies	. . . .	24
over 30 copies	. . . .	62

(4) Prepared to buy, but number not specified accounted for another

63 returns, and 8 of these are potentially very large purchases by the Canadian market.

These can be estimated to amount to the following sum 1,500

(5) Category in which need for the books was most felt:

Fiction	....	14
Non-Fiction	....	12
Fiction and Non-Fiction	....	278

(not all respondents indicated their opinions on this)

(6) Category of child who would benefit from the books:

Slow learners	....	321
Deaf	....	244
Mentally handicapped	....	234
Ethnic minority groups	....	194
Partially sighted	....	157
Normal children	....	117

'Other' was defined in several ways, as follows:

Language retarded
Language disordered
Language delayed
Speech and language handicapped
Specific language disordered
Aphasic
Dyslexic
Defective language problems
Communication handicapped (normal intelligence)
Emotionally disturbed
Maladjusted
Deprived
Autistic
Perceptive damaged
Dual & multiple handicapped
Adult stroke patients
Adult illiterates
Preschool

(7) Category of person replying:

Teachers (mainly in special schools)	....	223
Librarians (both general & children's)	....	72
Parents of handicapped children	....	40
Speech Therapists	....	34
Representatives of charities & other organizations	....	17
Other	....	11

Other occupations were as follows:

Lecturers in education	....	4
Social workers	....	2

plus one each of the following:

Head of Dyslexia Clinic
Warden of a special school
Head of centre for autistic children

MARKET RESEARCH–continued

Adult literacy co-ordinator
Senior adviser in an education department
Audiologist
Superintendent of special education in a Board of Education

(8) The number of replies received from other countries outside the UK is given below:

Canada	45
Australia	2

Appendix 4

Library facilities for physically and mentally handicapped children in Yorkshire

QUESTIONNAIRE TO CHIEF LIBRARIANS IN YORKSHIRE

1 Are there materials you provide specially for handicapped children?
Please list below:

2 At how many service points are handicapped children *specially* catered for?
3 How many staff have a *special* responsibility for the handicapped?
4 How many of the other staff are *specially* trained or experienced in work with handicapped children?
5 Please describe any *special* activities for handicapped children.
6 Please describe any *special* designs or adaptations of your library buildings for the convenience of the handicapped (e.g. ramps, lifts).
7 Please list any equipment provided specifically for the use of the handicapped (e.g. page turners, rests, stethosets).
8 Please list any items of such equipment to which you provide access (e.g. through the Social Service Department).
9 Please describe any deposit collections you provide for handicapped children (e.g. type of institution, size of collection, frequency materials are changed).
10 Please describe any home delivery service to handicapped children (e.g. numbers, frequency, etc.).
11 Please list any bodies concerned with handicapped children in your community. Ring those with whom you liaise.

12 In view of the financial climate do you think the authority would support services to handicapped children as a special need?

YES

NO

Please return the completed questionnaire to:

Mrs M. R. Marshall, Youth Libraries Group c/o 28 Park Place Leeds LS1 2SY by 19 December.

Appendix 5

Library facilities for physically and mentally handicapped children in Yorkshire

QUESTIONNAIRE TO SOCIETIES FOR HANDICAPPED CHILDREN

1 Do you think the Public Library should provide special services to handicapped children? (Please ring the answer which applies).

YES
NO

2 If YES, please ring which of these materials you would like the Public Library to provide for these children.

Talking books
Large Print Books
Toys

Please list any other materials you think could be provided.

3 Are there any special activities which you think could be organized by the library for these children? (e.g. story sessions, films etc.).

4 Please describe any special designs or adaptations of library buildings which would assist these children (e.g. ramps, lifts).

5 Please describe any special equipment which could be provided in the library for these children (e.g. page turners, rests, stethosets, etc.).

6 Please specify any institutions or societies for handicapped children who would find it useful to have collections of materials on loan from the Public Library.

7 Would a delivery service of materials from the library to individual homes of handicapped children be useful? (Please ring the answer which applies).

YES
NO

8 Are there any other services you think the Public Library could usefully provide for handicapped children?

9 Would your society be willing to contribute to a two-way exchange of information and advice on library provision for the handicapped children? (Please ring the answer which applies).

YES

NO

Please return the completed questionnaire to:
Mrs M. R. Marshall, Youth Libraries Group, c/o 28 Park Place Leeds LS1 2SY by 19 December.

Winkworth, Fay and Sunderland, Helen. *Public Library Facilities for Handicapped Children in Yorkshire: survey and directory*. Leeds: Library Association, Youth Libraries Group, Yorkshire Branch, 1976.

Bibliography

The titles of individual children's books referred to in the text are not cited here unless quoted from, as publication details, and even titles, vary between countries. However, an author reference appears in the general index.

The entries listed in the bibliography are of print sources used in the course of research for the book.

BOOKS

Adamson, Jean and Gareth. *Topsy and Tim at School.* London: Blackie and Home Library for the Deaf, 1968.

Ahrens, Michael and Stott, Grant. *Activities for Intellectually Handicapped Children: a handbook for parents and friends.* New Zealand: Whitcoulls, 1975.

American Library Association. *Standards for Library Services for the Blind and Visually Handicapped.* Chicago: ALA, 1967.

Association for Spina Bifida and Hydrocephalus. *Children with Spina Bifida in School: a booklet for teachers and students.* London: ASBH, 1978.

Baker, Augusta and Greene, Ellin. *Storytelling: art and technique.* New York: Bowker, 1978.

Banting, P. *The design of Clapham Park School for the Partially Sighted. In* Library Association. *Clear Print.* London: LA, 1971, pp. 16–23.

Baranyay, Eileen. *A Lifetime of Learning: a survey of further education facilities for mentally handicapped adolescents and adults.* London: National Society for Mentally Handicapped Children, 1976.

Baskin, B. H. and Harris, K. (eds.) *The Special Child in the Library.* Chicago: ALA, 1976.

Bell, Peter. *Basic Teaching for Slow Learners.* London: Muller Educational, 1970.

Bliss, C. K. *Semantography-Blissymbolics.* Sydney: C. K. Bliss, PO Box 222, Coogee, Sydney, Australia.

Bliss, C. K. and McNaughton, S. The book to the film *Mr Symbol Man.* Canada: National Film Board of Canada and Australia, 1974.

Bloom, B. S. Mastery of learning and its implication for curriculum development. *In* Golby, M (ed.) *Curriculum Development.* London: Croom Helm, 1975, pp. 334–50.

Bloom, Freddy. *The Boy who Couldn't Hear.* London: Bodley Head, 1977.

Blythman, Marion (ed.) *Let's Go Workbook Kit.* Published in conjunction with BBC TV's series *Let's Go.* Edinburgh: Scottish Health Education Unit and National Society for Mentally Handicapped Children, n.d.

Boocock, Sarane S. *An Introduction to the Sociology of Learning.* Boston: Houghton Mifflin, 1972.

Braf, Per-Gunnar. *The Physical Environment and the Visually Handicapped.* Sweden, ICTA Information Centre, Fack, S–16103, Brooma 3, 1974.

Bramley, Gerald. *Outreach: library services for the institutionalized, the elderly and the physically handicapped.* London: Bingley, 1978.

Brennan, Mary. *Can Deaf Children Acquire Language? An evaluation of linguistic principles in deaf education.* London: British Deaf Association, 1976.

British Association of Teachers of the Deaf. *Help: a collection of articles for teachers new to the education of hearing impaired children.* Bolton: BATD, n.d.

British Broadcasting Corporation. *In Touch: aids and services for blind and partially sighted people.* London: BBC, rev. edn. 1977.

British Psychological Society. *Children in Hospitals for the Subnormal: report.* London: British Psychological Society, 1966.

Bunch, Antonia J. and Cumming, Eileen E. *Libraries in Hospitals: a review of services in Scotland.* Edinburgh: Scottish Hospital Centre. 1969.

Butler, Dorothy. *Cushla and Her Books.* London: Hodder and Stoughton, 1979.

Cass, Hilary and Stone, Karen. *Take Six Children.* London: National Society for Mentally Handicapped Children, 1978.

Chapman, E. K. *Visually Handicapped Children and Young People.* London: Routledge and Kegan Paul, 1978.

Charlip, Remy and Beth, Mary. *Handtalk: an ABC of finger spelling and sign language.* New York: Parents, 1974.

Cleugh, M. F. *Teaching the Slow Learner in the Primary School.* London: Methuen, 1961.

College of Speech Therapists. *Communication Charts for the Severely Speech and Language Handicapped.* London: College of Speech Therapists, n.d.

Corbett, Anne. *The Librarian's Choice.* London: HMSO, 1978.

Corey, Patricia Blair. *School Library Services for Deaf Children.* Washington D.C.: Alexander Graham Bell Association, 1960.

Critchley, Macdonald. *The Dyslexic Child.* London: Heinemann Medical, 1969.

Cumming, Eileen E. *Hospital and Welfare Library Services: an international bibliography.* London: Library Association, 1978.

Cylke, F. K. *Library Services for the Blind and Physically Handicapped.* Munich: Saur, 1979.

Denton, David M. *The Philosophy of Total Communication.* London: British Deaf Association, 1976.

Department of Education and Science. *Education (Handicapped Children) Act 1970.* Chapter 52. London: HMSO, 1970.

Department of Education and Science. *Education (Mentally Handicapped Children) (Scotland) Act 1974.* Chapter 27. London: HMSO, 1974.

Department of Education and Science. *Education of Children in Hospitals for the Mentally Handicapped.* HMI Series: Matters for Discussion. London: HMSO, 1979.

Department of Education and Science. *Education for the Visually Handicapped: report of the Vernon Committee.* London: HMSO, 1972.

Department of Education and Science. *Education Statistics for the United Kingdom, 1975.* London: HMSO, 1978.

Department of Education and Science. *List of Special Schools for Handicapped Pupils in England and Wales.* London: HMSO, 1969.

Dickman, Irving R. *et. al. Sex Education and Family Life for Visually Handicapped Children and Youth: a resource guide.* New York: Human Sciences Press, 1975.

Disabled Living Foundation. *The Disabled Schoolchild and Kitchen Sense.* London: Heinemann Health Books, 1976.

Dwyer, Annie C. *et. al. South Australian Toy Libraries: a survey 1976.* Adelaide: South Australia Institute of Technology, 1976.

Everard, Margaret P. *An Approach to Teaching Autistic Children.* London: Pergamon, 1976.

Freeman, Peggy. *Understanding the Deaf-Blind Child.* London: Heinemann Health Books, 1975.

Furneaux, Barbara. *The Special Child.* 2nd edn. London: Penguin, 1973.

Going, Mona E. (comp.) *Hospital Libraries and Work with the Disabled,* London: Library Association, 1963.

Golby, Michael (ed.) *Curriculum Development.* London: Croom Helm, 1975.

Goldstein, Henry (ed.). *Readings in . . .* Series covering autism, deaf education, mental retardation, physical handicap, speech and hearing impairment, visual handicap. New York: Special Learning Corporation, 1978.

Gulliford, Ronald and Widlake, Paul. *Teaching Materials for Disadvantaged Children.* Schools Council Curriculum Bulletin 5. London: Evans/Methuen Educational, 1974.

Guralnick, Michael J. (ed.) *Early Intervention and the Integration of Handicapped and Non-Handicapped Children.* Baltimore, Maryland: University Park Press, 1978.

Hallas, Charles H. *The Care and Training of the Mentally Subnormal.* Bristol: Wright, 1978.

Halliday, Carol. *The Visually Impaired Child: growth, learning and development, infancy to school age.* Louisville, Kentucky: American Printing House for the Blind, 1970.

Hannam, Charles. *Parents and Mentally Handicapped Children.* London: Penguin, 1975.

Haskell, Simon H., Barrett, Elizabeth K. and Taylor, Helen. *The Education of Motor and Neurologically Handicapped Children.* London: Croom Helm, 1977.

International Federation of Library Associations. Hospital Libraries Section. *Organization, Description of Work and Statistics of Library Services in Hospitals and Institutions for the Handicapped: results of a questionnaire received from members of IFLA section.* IFLA, 1977.

International Year of the Child Secretariat. *Should Prevention of Blindness Be Your Emphasis for IYC?* IYC report no. 9. New York: IYC, April, 1978.

Jensen, Virginia Allan and Haller, Dorcas Woodbury. *What's That?* Denmark: Forlaget IBIS, 1977 and London: Collins, 1979.

Jobling, Megan and Parfit, Jessie. *How to Set Up a Resource Centre on Handicap.* London: Institute for Research into Mental and Multiple Handicap, 1977.

Kirk, Samuel A. and Johnson, G. Orville. *Educating the Retarded Child.* Boston: Houghton Mifflin, 1951.

Kirman, Brian. *Mental Handicap: a brief guide.* London: Crosby Lockwood Staples, 1979.

Koestler, Frances A. (ed.) *COMSTAC Report: standards for strengthened services.* New York: Commission on Standards and Accreditation of Services to the Blind, 1962.

Lancaster-Gaye, S. (ed.) *Personal Relationships: the handicapped and the community.* London: Routledge and Kegan Paul, 1972.

Large Type Books in Print, 1978. New York: Bowker, 1978.

Leeming, K. and others. *Education for Severely Educationally Subnormal Pupils: teaching language and communication to the mentally handicapped.* London: National Foundation for Educational Research, 1977.

Lewis, Joy. *Libraries for the Handicapped.* Pamphlet 33. London: Library Association, 1969.

Library Association. *Clear Print: papers and proceedings of a conference.* London: LA, 1972.

Library Association. *Library Resource Provision in Schools: recommended guidelines.* London: LA, 1978.

Library Association and the National Association for the Education of the Partially Sighted. *Print for the Visually Handicapped Reader: paper and proceedings of a conference 1970.* LA Publication no. 6. London: LA, 1971.

Library Association, Youth Libraries Group. *Storytelling: a collection of papers on aspects of storytelling and reading, by experienced storytellers.* London: LA, Youth Libraries Group, 1979.

Lock, R. N. (ed.) *Manual of Library Economy.* London: Bingley, 1977.

London Head Teachers Association. *The Integration Argument.* London: LHTA, n.d.

Loring, James. *Teaching the Cerebral Palsied Child.* London: Spastics Society and Heinemann, 1965.

Lowenfield, Berthold (ed.) *The Visually Handicapped Child in School,* New York: Day, 1973.

McNaughton, S., *et. al. Teaching Guidelines.* Toronto: Blissymbolic Communication Foundation, 1975.

Marshall, Margaret R. Children's libraries. *In* Lock, R. N., *op. cit.,* Chapter 12.

Marshall, Margaret R. (comp.) *Each According to his Ability: a list of books and other visual material for use by and with mentally handicapped children.* Oxford: School Library Association, 1975.

Marshall, Margaret R. *Libraries and Literature for Teenagers.* London: Deutsch, 1975.

Marshall, Margaret R. (comp.) *Seeing Clear: books for the partially sighted child.* Oxford: School Library Association, 1977.

Martin, W. J. Handicapped readers. *In* Lock, R. N., *op. cit.,* Chapter 13.

Merrill, Edward C. *The Responsibility of Professionals to the Deaf Consumer.* London: British Deaf Association, 1976.

Mindel, Eugene D. and Vernon, McCoy. *They Grow in Silence: the deaf child and his family.* Maryland: National Association of the Deaf, 1976.

Money, John. *The Disabled Reader – Education for the Dyslexic Child.* Baltimore: John Hopkins Press, 1966.

Moody, M. T. and Limper, M. K. *Bibliotherapy: methods and materials.* Chicago: ALA/AHIL, 1971.

National Accreditation Council for Agencies Serving the Blind and Visually Handicapped. *Standards for Production of Reading Materials for the Blind and Visually Handicapped.* New York: NACASBVH, 1970.

National Association for the Education of the Partially Sighted. *Partially Sighted Children: a summary of their needs and existing provision.* London: NAEPS, 1972.

National Association of Hospital Teachers. *Hospital Schools in England and Wales: report.* London: NAHT, 1976.

National College of Teachers of the Deaf and Society of Teachers of the Deaf. *The Hearing Impaired Child in Your Class.* London: NCTD and STD, 1976.

National Union of Teachers. *Teaching in Hospital Schools.* London: NUT, 1973.

Newman, Janet (comp.). *Sex Education: a critical evaluation of material.* Pamphlet no. 20. London: Library Association, Youth Libraries Group, 1979.

Office of Population Censuses and Surveys. Social Survey Part 1. *Handicapped and Impaired in Great Britain* London: HMSO, 1971.

Open University. *The Handicapped Person in the Community.* Milton Keynes: Open University, 1975.

Ørjasæter, Tordis. *Boka on Dag Tore.* Oslo: Cappelens, 1976.

Parfit, Jessie. *Emotional Disturbance in Handicapped Children.* Highlight no. 9. London: National Children's Bureau, 1974.

Parfit, Jessie and Jobling, M. *IRMMH Research Centre on Handicap in Children: final report on the experimental project.* London: Institute for Research into Mental and Multiple Handicap, 1977.

Parlett, Malcolm. *Towards Integration: a study of blind and partially sighted children in ordinary schools.* London: National Foundation for Educational Research, 1976.

Phinney, Eleanor. *The Library and the Patient: an introduction to library services for patients in health care institutions.* Chicago: ALA, 1977.

Pilling, Dora. *The Child with Cerebral Palsy.* London: National Foundation for Educational Research and National Children's Bureau, 1973.

Pilling, Dora. *The Child with Spina Bifida.* London: National Foundation for Educational Research and National Children's Bureau, 1973.

Pilling, Dora. *The Handicapped Child: research review.* Vol. 3. London: Longman (for National Children's Bureau), 1973.

Prentiss, Sam. *Improving Library Services to the Blind, Partially Sighted and Physically Handicapped in New York State: a report.* New York: Assistant Commissioner for Libraries. University of the State of New York, 1973.

Redfern, Margaret (ed.) *New Readers Start Here.* London: Library Association, 1975.

Rowlands, Peter. *The Fugitive Mind: the early development of an autistic child.* London: Dent, 1976.

Rutter, M. *Children with Delayed Speech.* London: Heinemann, 1972.

Schauder, Donald E. and Cram, Malcolm D. *Libraries for the Blind: an international study of policies and practices.* Sheffield: Peter Peregrinus, 1977.

Scottish Home and Health Department and Scottish Education

Department. *A Better Life: report on services for the mentally handicapped in Scotland.* Edinburgh: HMSO, 1979.

Segal, Stanley (comp.) *Books for the Teachers of Children with Learning Difficulties.* London: National Book League, 1979.

Shaw, Alison. *Print for Partial Sight: a report to the Library Association Sub-Committee on books for readers with defective sight.* London: Library Association, 1969.

Smith, Sally L. *The Hearing Disabled Children: who are they and how do we teach them?* Discussion paper on themes related to IYC. New York: International Year of the Child Secretariat, 1979.

Stevens, M. *Education and Social Needs of Children with Severe Handicap.* London: Edward Arnold, 1976.

Stone, J. and Taylor, F. *Handbook for Parents with a Handicapped Child.* Home and School Council. Billericay: CASE Publications, 1972.

Strom, Maryalls G. (ed.) *Library Service to the Blind and Physically Handicapped.* New Jersey: Scarecrow, 1977.

Toy Libraries Association. *Toys for Children with Hearing, Speech and Language Difficulties.* London: Toy Libraries Association, 1975.

Vernon, M. D. *The Psychology of Perception.* London: Penguin, 1962.

Vernon, McCoy. *Total Communication: the human right of deaf children and their families.* London: British Deaf Association, 1974.

Vipont, Elfrida and Briggs, Raymond. *The Elephant and the Bad Baby.* London: Hamish Hamilton, 1968.

Warnock, Mary. *Educating the Handicapped: evidence submitted to the Committee of Inquiry into the education and other needs of handicapped children and young persons.* London: NUT, 1975.

Warnock, Mary. *Special Educational Needs: report of the Committee of Enquiry into the education of handicapped children and young people.* London: HMSO, 1978.

Winkworth, Fay and Sunderland, Helen. *Public Library Facilities for Handicapped Children in Yorkshire: survey and directory.* Leeds: Library Association, Youth Libraries Group, Yorkshire Branch, 1976.

World Federation of the Deaf. *International Sign Language of the Deaf: 'Gestumo'* London: British Deaf Association, 1975.

Younghusband, E. *et. al. Living with Handicap.* London: National Children's Bureau, 1970.

PERIODICAL ARTICLES

Adamescu, Vasile. How do I perceive the world? *Braille Review*, no. 4, 1973. Viata Nova appendix.

Atinma, Moraye I. Public and school library services to the physically handicapped in Nigeria: an evaluation. *International Library Review*, vol. 1, no. 4, October 1979, pp. 441–49.

Bennett, Janet M. The library: the retarded person's alternative. *Catholic Library World*, vol. 45, no. 9, April 1974, pp. 420–22.

Braille Book Review, bi-monthly article and letters and annotated entries.

Carnett, Jean. Towards integration: special children in a comprehensive school. *Rathbone News*, June 1977, pp. 45–9.

Casey, G. M. Library services to the handicapped and institutionalized. *Library Trends*, vol. 20, no. 2, October 1971, pp. 350–66.

Champlin, J. L. and C. J. Telling simple stories with retarded adults. *Catholic Library World*, no. 48, March 1977, pp. 322–27.

Cumming, Eileen E. Children in hospital: do they need a library service? *Book Trolley*, vol. 3, no. 3, September 1971, pp. 3–9.

Cumming, Eileen E. Reading for the mentally handicapped: a selective bibliography. *Book Trolley*, vol. 3, no. 5, March 1972, pp. 14–15.

Davison, Mary B. Libraries in hospital schools. *National Froebel Foundation Bulletin*, June 1961, pp. 10–12.

Dresang, Eliza T. There are no other children. *School Library Journal*, September 1977, pp. 19–23.

Freytag, Gisela. Bibliotherapy by means of picture books for speech handicapped children. *International Library Review*, vol. 9, no. 2, 1977, pp. 197–203.

Gallimore, J. E. Criteria for the selection and evaluation of book and non-book materials for mentally retarded adolescents and adults. Thesis. San Jose: California State University, 1973.

Gray, Sally *et. al.* Sally and company are leaving. *Link* September/October 1975, pp. 8–9.

Groff, P. Children's fiction and the psychology of deafness. *School Librarian*, vol. 24, no. 3, September 1976, pp. 191–202.

Guldager, Virginia. Communication and the multiply handicapped child. Perkins School for the Blind, Watertown, Massachusetts (mimeo).

Happ, W. William. Multi-media services for retardees in institutions. *Top of the News*, vol. 25, no. 3, April 1969, p. 268.

Harris, N. G. Audio-visual resources: resident library services for the mentally retarded. *AHIL Quarterly*, no. 11, Spring 1971, pp. 35–8.

Hay, Wendy. Books in care: visiting Lambeth's Special Care Unit. *Assistant Librarian*, vol. 69, nos. 7/8, July/August 1976, pp. 134–5.

Heie, Bjørg. Literature and library services for the handicapped in Norway. *Scandinavian Public Libraries Quarterly*, vol. 9, nos. 3/4, 1976, pp. 192–7.

Henne, J. F. Serving visually handicapped children. *School Library Journal*, December 1978, pp. 36–7.

Hill, Janet. Playgroup for mentally handicapped children. *Hertfordshire County Library Newsletter*, 1976.

Hopkinson, R. G. Lighting in schools for the visually handicapped. *Light and Lighting*, no. 66, September 1973, pp. 262–65.

Hunsicker, Marya. When the blind begin to read. *School Library Journal*, November 1972, pp. 79–81.

Hunsucker, Coy Kate. Public library services to blind and physically handicapped children. *Health and Rehabilitative Library Services Division Journal*, vol. 2, no. 2, February 1976, p. 43.

Jensen, Joanne C. The library and the deaf child. *Catholic Library World*, vol. 45, no. 9, April 1974, pp. 426–28.

Jerrolds, Bob. Preparing librarians to help the disabled reader. *Wilson Library Bulletin*, May 1976, p. 719.

Johnson, Elizabeth and Merriweather, Thelma. Blind children learn to relate. *American Libraries*, vol. 1, February 1970, pp. 168–9.

Library Association, Hospital Libraries Group. Sick and handicapped children: report of a joint meeting with the Youth Libraries Group held at Great Ormond Street Hospital, 1973. *Health and Welfare Libraries Quarterly*, vol. 1, no. 1, March 1974, pp. 12–13.

Limper, Hilda K. Serving mentally retarded children in our libraries. *Catholic Library World*, vol. 45, no. 9, April 1974, pp. 423–5.

Marais, Elizabeth. Opening doors only to close them? *Times Educational Supplement*, 21 September 1978, p. 47.

Marshall, Margaret R. The children's librarian and the handicapped child. *International Library Review*, no. 9, 1977, pp. 183–96.

Matthews, Geraldine M. Institutionalized children's needs. *Library Trends*, Winter 1978, pp. 371–88.

Miller, Russell. Unlocking the doors. *Sunday Times Colour Supplement*, 13 March 1977, pp. 32–42.

Montgomery, Helen. Special report: outreach to the retarded. *Wilson Library Bulletin*, vol. 50, no. 9, May 1976, pp. 688–90.

Mulhern, Kevin. Among the sighted. *Times Educational Supplement*, 22 September 1978, p. 46.

Ohio Media Spectrum, vol. 30, no. 1, 1978. 20 articles on the special child, pp. 4–73.

Paton, Xenia. Teaching the mentally retarded to read: some personal experiences. *Book Trolley*, vol. 3, no. 5, March 1972, pp. 9–11.

Philadelphia Public Library, *ALA Bulletin*, vol. 55, no. 4, April 1961, p. 320.

Pill, R. and Jacobs, R. Report on a pilot study on the problems of long-stay children in hospital. University of Swansea, 1974 (mimeo).

Polack, Margaret. Bringing up Ruth. *Parents Voice*, vol. 25, no. 1, March 1975, pp. 24–5.

Rensberger, Boyce. For the deaf the language gap is unbridgeable. *New York Times*, 22 April 1979, p. 29.

Robertson, Mary Lett. Materials, programs suggestions for hearing impaired children. *School Media Quarterly*, vol. 4, no. 3, Spring 1976. pp. 263–68.

Russell, Jean. Hospital storytelling for children. *Book Trolley*, vol. 3, no. 8, December 1972, pp. 7–9.

Secker, Leonora. Sex education and mental handicap. *Special Education*, vol. 62, no. 1, March 1973, pp. 27–8.

Shropshire, Florence G. Why is it better to have a library for the blind in an agency for the blind rather than any other setting? *Braille Monitor*, March–April 1977, pp. 107–9.

Simpson, Ray D. Books for children with limited vision. *Ontario Library Review*, vol. 55, no. 2, 1971, pp. 128–40.

Smith, Charles. A toy library for handicapped children. *Australian Library Journal*, vol. 25, no. 4, May 1976, pp. 142–44.

Unesco Bulletin for Libraries, vol. 26, no. 3, May/June 1972, pp. 129–31.

Vellerman, Ruth A. The school library in the education of handicapped children. *Rehabilitation Literature*, vol. 32, no. 5, May 1971, pp. 138–40.

Weber, Hans. Kinderliteratur fur das behinderte Kind. *Lernbehinderte Kinder*, Jg. 1, 1968, HI.

Wire, Catherine B. Books for children who read by touch and sound. *Quarterly Journal of the Library of Congress*, vol. 30, no. 2, April 1973, pp. 159–64.

Wilson Library Bulletin, vol. 50, no. 9, May 1976, pp. 704–38. Special issue.

Wollman, D. C. and Hickmott, Joan. Language development for deaf pupils. *Dialogue*, Schools Council Newsletter, no. 23, 1976, pp. 6–7.

Zerface, W. A. Hire the handicapped librarian. *Wilson Library Bulletin*, April 1977, pp. 656–60.

Index